Women's Glib

A Collection of Women's Humor

Edited by
Rosalind Warren

The Crossing Press
Freedom, CA 95019

Dedicated To My Husband, the Feminist

The Editor wishes to thank:

Mom and Dad, without whom I wouldn't have a sense of humor. Alvia Crooks, without whom I'd have an entirely different sense of humor. My sister Diane, for giving me someone to laugh with (and only occasionally at) during my formative years (which are still ongoing). Dorothy Parker, Nicole Hollander and Emma Peel, for inspiration. Terry Gross, for Fresh Air. Mameve Medwed, the world's best writing teacher. Linda Angelo, for the title Women's Glib. Humor Gurus Savoy Rose Jade, John Mort and Mike Walsh. The ridiculously patient staff of the Bala Cynwyd Public Library. Former funny friends Joan Helfman, Lisse Palmer and Linda Diamond—where are you now?? The Women's Glib Ad Hoc Humor Collecting Collective (Lawrence Blum, Diane Blum, Kate Stone, Daniel Blum, Ann Collette and Jody Worden). I'd like to thank Maggee Page Harriz, my massage therapist, for putting up with my yakking, kvetching and crowing about this book when I should have been relaxing and breathing deeply. Thanks, Anne Elizabeth Beidler, for everything, especially the photo. I would also like to mention that my life has taken on new meaning since I accepted Irene Zahava as my personal savior. A million thanks to Deek, and to Elaine Goldman Gill. Thanks also to my husband, Richard Charles Smith, who followed me to a new town, leaving friends and family behind, considers our baby equally his in terms of responsibility and care, and gives me the same tenderness and nurturing (better tenderness and nurturing, probably) that I give him. Lastly, I'd like to thank Irene Calvo and Barb Straus, and also D.J.W. Blum, Ph.D., P.E., my trusty consultant in the area of waste water treatment.

Cover art and design by Nicole Hollander

Printed in the U.S.A

Library of Congress Cataloging in Publication Data

Women's Glib: A Collection of Women's Humor / edited by Rosalind Warren.
p. cm.
ISBN 0-89594-470-7 – ISBN 0-89594-466-9 (pbk)
1. Feminism–Humor. 2. Women–Humor. I. Warren, Rosalind, 1954-
PN6231.F44W66 1991
817.008'09287–dc20   91-7498
                                        CIP

CONTENTS

DEAR READER:

I put this book together for a laugh. A woman's laugh.

Every other humor collection I've read has been made up almost entirely of work by men, with maybe one or two pieces by women thrown in. Something by Dorothy Parker. That piece Nora Ephron wrote about her breasts back in the sixties. And it's a *terrific* story, but if I read Eudora Welty's "Why I Live at the P.O." one more time I'm going to throw up.

Reading these books you'd never know there were so many wonderful, hilarious (not to mention feminist) women humorists. So what I've done is gather together the work of 70 of them. *Women's Glib* includes material by well-known humorists like Nicole Hollander, Roz Chast, Alison Bechdel, Claire Bretecher, Lynda Barry and Alice Kahn. In addition there are relative newcomers like Julie Blackwomon, Marcia Steil and Noreen Stevens. There are writers and artists whose work has gained loyal local followings but is not yet widely known, like Myra Chanin (Philly's "Mother Wonderful") and Ellen Orleans. Plus contributions by women such as Maya Angelou and Lesléa Newman, who aren't humorists but who occasionally toss off a funny gem.

The topics covered range from Cher to gefilte fish, from panty angst to the Pope. Including God, childbirth, going out, breaking up, death, sex and President Bush. And, of course, a visit to the gynecologist. (And a visit to the abortionist—perhaps the toughest subject for humor).

What I sought (and found, I believe) is what one writer called "guffaw humor." Not just the kind of piece that'll make you grin, but the kind that'll knock you off your chair laughing.

The kind of book that's very difficult to quietly read in the library.

The kind of book you can't *possibly* read eating lunch.

Men will find some of the material in *Women's Glib* funny.

Men will find some of it incomprehensible.

Men may even find some of this material offensive. (So, for that matter, may some women).

I can live with that.

My hope is that *you* will laugh out loud reading *Women's Glib*. Often. If you like it, there will be more.*

Enjoy!

ROZ WARREN

* I'm already gathering material for the "sequel"—*Women's Glibber*. If you're funny or know someone who is, I want to hear from you at P.O. Box 259, Bala Cynwyd, PA 19004.

MORSELS AND MEMORIES

? WHAT IS...

YOUR PHILOSOPHICAL OUTLOOK?

#1. You wander alone down a crowded city street. Jostled in the bustle, solitary yet surrounded, you think: "These people are...

A. My brothers. My sisters.

B. Perverts. Probably pick-axe murderers.

C. I sure could go for a chili-dog...

2. Amid the crowd, a stranger slowly turns. As his eyes meet yours, you muse:

A. I know what he feels. He feels hope. He feels fear.

B. Why's that pervert looking at ME?

C. Maybe a pepperoni pizza with olives...

Science has noted three basic types.

3. The stranger approaches. He is near! Instinctively, you grab:

A. His hand.

B. A can of mace.

C. An ice cream cone from a vendor.

4. With all your heart, you cry out loud:

A. Put away your fears, my friend!

B. Put down that pick-axe, you pervert!

C. Put some chocolate sprinkles on top..

5. Further down, construction workers are tearing the street to rubble. "How symbolic!" you marvel, "It reminds me of...

A. The Path of Life.

B. The Highway to Hell.

C. Rocky Road. My favorite flavor...

RESULTS

IF MOST OF YOUR ANSWERS WERE:

A. You are an OPTIMIST. You see Life as a source of companionship and joy.

B. You are a PESSIMIST. You see Life as a source of threat and misery.

C. You are a GASTRONOMIST. You see Life as a source of really great things to eat.

© 1988 MARIAN HENLEY

MARIAN HENLEY

Morsels and Memories
My late mother's 21 steps to the proper preparation of gefilte fish.

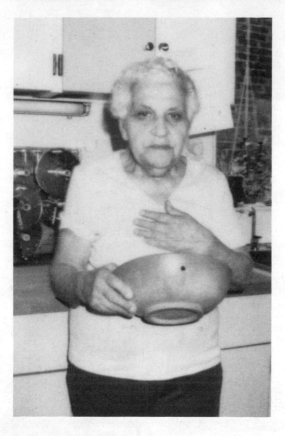

1 Two weeks before a major Jewish holiday, call your daughter and ask her what she plans to serve at the festive meal. Express your outrage when she suggests serving doctored up canned gefilte fish. Offer to make the fish yourself.

2 Suggest that your daughter take a day off from work so that she can watch you make the fish, so she'll know how to do it for her kids after she has put you in The Home. Two days before the holiday, call your daughter and tell her you hate to disappoint her, but you simply don't have the strength to make gefilte fish.

3 While your daughter is racing all over looking for a substitute appetizer, get all dressed up and take a bus...and a subway...and another bus...

4 ... to an obscure fish store in a slum where they still sell LIVE CARP.

5 Examine the carp swimming around in the fish tank. Ask the owner if any fresher carp will be arriving soon.

6 On principle, reject the first two fish that he offers you.

7 Accept the third or fourth. Allow him to fillet and skin the carp, but NEVER let him put your fish near his electric grinder. Far be it for you to accuse anyone unjustly, but you know he has ground dead carp in it.

8 Lugging three heavy shopping bags filled with fish, take three buses home, unless someone has told you about a way of taking four.

9 Call your daughter and tell her that you felt a little bit better and decided to go to your special fish store and pick up the carp. You know how busy she is right before the holidays so you didn't want to ask her to drive all the way out there.

10 Tell her how exhausted you are and describe in detail the assassin who tried to steal your pocketbook as you were boarding the second bus. Inquire whether your daughter would mind picking you up. You wouldn't normally ask, but it's much easier to make the gefilte fish in her kitchen because she has all the latest electric gadgets.

11 Remove several washed mixing bowls from your daughter's dishwasher and rinse them to make sure they are clean.

12 There should be a separate bowl for each ingredient so that dirt from the carrots will not get on the celery. Put the diced carrots in one bowl, the sliced celery in the second, the chopped onions in the third and then combine them all in a fourth bowl. Ask your daughter to stop whatever she's doing and come and watch you.

13 Eye your daughter's food processor with suspicion. Ask her to help you operate it. Chop the carp in it for 15 seconds, then move all the ingredients into your ancient wooden chopping bowl.

14 Rev up those Hadassah arms and attack the ingredients with a dull bladed *hockmesser* for 90 minutes. Demand that your daughter acknowledge the superiority of your withered arm over a horsepower motor.

15 Place your hand on your chest and moan. Accept your daughter's offer to help. Give her the bowl and the *hockmesser*.

16 Twelve seconds later, snatch the bowl and chopper out of your daughter's hands. Tell her to watch carefully so she'll be more of a help next year. Pulverize the fish with your chopper for another 52 minutes.

17 On the bottom of a cast-iron pot with a non-matching lid (rescued by your mother during a pogrom and brought in steerage to America), arrange slices of carrots, onions, celery, fish heads, skin and bones.

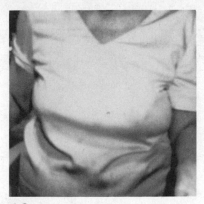

18 Form the chopped fish mush into oval patties and lay them gently on top of the ingredients in the pot.

19 Add liquid and seasonings, bring to a boil, lower to simmer, cover the pot and let the fish cook until they're ready and taste good . . . but not as good as last year's.

20 After the patties cool, arrange them on a beautiful serving platter for your daughter and her guests. Dump the heads, skin and bones in a chipped soup bowl for yourself. Practice saying that the heads and the bones are the tastiest portions until you sound convincing.

21 The morning after the holiday, call your daughter and tell her that you just tasted a piece of bottled fish that was even more delicious than what she served last night. Tell her it's a shame she made it from scratch when everyone does such wonderful things with canned.

MYRA CHANIN

KATE GAWF

Anorex
a commercial message

Have you tried everything to lose weight? Diet plans, exercisers, inflatable suits? Did you have your teeth wired? Do you force yourself to throw up after every meal, and find that you're still gaining three to five pounds a week? Are you thinking of buying a meat cleaver?

Before you do anything you'll regret, try ANOREX. Yes, ANOREX, a simple little diet pill that works, not on your fat, but on your mind.

For years, scientists have been working nights and weekends to come up with a formula to take the joy out of cooking. And eating. Their painstaking research has finally paid off—with a revolutionary breakthrough in the field of dietetics. No gimmicks, no frills, no diets, and here's the best part: no painful exercise.

With ANOREX you'll be convinced that you simply aren't hungry. Food will lose all meaning. You won't even remember what your mouth is for. You'll be able to take weight off and keep it off.

In just a few short weeks on the ANOREX plan, you can become as emaciated as any Vogue model, drug addict, or terminal cancer patient. You'll never want to see another pork chop, another coconut cake, another hot fudge sundae. For as long as you can still walk, you'll be able to leave your home and go anywhere, secure in the knowledge that you'll never eat again. For the first time, you'll see bones you never knew you had.

Sound like a miracle? Too good to be true? Then let me speak from personal experience: I've been on the ANOREX plan for fourteen days, and already I can see and feel the results. I'm almost too weak to tell you any more about it.

What have you got to lose? Plenty. And for a limited time only, we'll send you a 30-day supply of ANOREX for just $19.95. That's right, $19.95, and the secret of fast and permanent weight loss can be yours for the asking.

And if you act now, we'll include absolutely free with your order a 50-page, colorfully illustrated ANOREX booklet filled with hundreds of disgusting suggestions about where food comes from, where it goes, and what it turns into . . .

Try ANOREX for just thirty days, and if you're not completely delighted with the results, have your next-of-kin return the empty ANOREX bottle for a full refund.

This is a very sick society, you know it and I know it, and if you look too healthy, you won't fit in—so order now. That's ANOREX, A-N-O-R-E-X, ANOREX.

When the real you just isn't right.

JULIA WILLIS

Good Candy, Bad Candy

Any kind of Hershey's chocolate is good, especially Hershey's kisses. Anything that comes in an individual wrapper, like butterscotch or lemon drops, is good. Life-savers are very good; best of all is a package of all cherry. Mint flavored life-savers are really medicine and should never be confused with candy. Licorice, if it's wrapped in plastic and doesn't come from the large glass container that sits on the counter in the candy store, is good, but black licorice tastes awful. Cake can sometimes be candy and is good as long as there is no chocolate: pound cake, cheese cake or cheese Danish. Vanilla wafer cookies and Graham crackers also fall into this category. For some reason, so do fig newtons.

All other candy is bad.

Any candy that is sold in a movie theater is bad and should be avoided at all costs, even if it looks exactly like candy you're allowed to eat when it's not bought in a movie theater. Any candy that comes from a machine, especially gum balls, malt balls, hot or sour balls and all-day suckers: bad. Little pastel dots that come on long strips of paper: bad. Pez, in any flavor, from any kind of dispenser: bad. Little wax bottles that you bite the tops off and suck the juice out of: bad. Ices of any kind, unless they're made from real juice, by your mother, and frozen in your own freezer at home: bad. Gum—any kind, any color, any flavor, even Chiclets: bad. Long strips of dried fruit, wrapped in a cylinder (even if it says Real Fruit on the wrapper): bad. Mars bars, Snickers, 3 Musketeers, Mr. Goodbar, Chunkies: all bad. Any kind of Easter candy, especially little chocolate eggs (not to be confused with good chocolate, which is only Hershey's): bad. Christmas candy, even candy-canes that come individually wrapped: bad. Halloween candy of any sort, no matter who gives it to you: bad. Any candy that tries to pretend it's something else, by being shaped like a peanut, a kernel of corn, a banana, a slice of watermelon, etc.: bad. Anything made out of wax, especially if it's shaped like a tongue or like lips: bad. Candy cigarettes: bad, bad, bad.

General guideline to be used whenever you're in doubt: if all your friends can eat it, it's probably bad. If no one else would want to eat it, it's probably good.

IRENE ZAHAVA

This is a Compliment?

You're incrediburgable
she said
which is to say
You're a little incredible
but a lot more like a
hamburger.

CHOCOLATE WATERS

PLAIN GEOMETRY WITH REAL FRUIT
ON THE BOTTOM

JENNIFER BERMAN

Preparing Dinner

I thought tuna fish salad would be alright. I didn't think anything would go wrong with tuna fish salad. I felt optimistic as I set the brown paper bag with the ingredients on the table.

I unpacked two small cans of tuna and placed them on the table with the mermaids face to face, tail to tail. Mermaids like that. They like to be close to each other. I took two small jars of mayonnaise out of the bag. I stood one on top of the other, head to head. Soon I would switch them around. Those who are on top shall be on the bottom. Those who are on the bottom shall be on top. I unpacked two boxes of raisins, dessert. I stood the two boxes of raisins on the table with the smiling buxom raisin maids looking at each other but not touching. Last, I took out a package of English muffins and placed the brown paper grocery bag on the floor to serve as a receptacle for garbage.

English muffins are my favorite food. Nothing can go wrong with English muffins, if you buy the presliced kind. But one should not be deceived. Certain brands claim to be presliced, but when you take them out of their plyo-film bag, and take them in your hands to separate the two partners, you find they are not presliced at all, but joined along an arc in their circumference like Siamese twins.

Separating Siamese twins is a delicate operation. Many things can go wrong. If one's hand s the least bit shaky, if one's eye is less than keen, if the surgical instrument is deflected even a hair's breadth, a chunk of flesh will be severed from its rightful owner and will remain adhering like a tumor upon the body of the other.

Of course the initial question is, 'Do the Siamese twins actually want to be separated?' They could conceivably prefer to travel through life, or in the case of an English muffin, to travel into the human mouth, as one indivisible unit. You can ask Siamese twins but you can't ask an English muffin. And that's the fundamental problem with food. You never know just what it wants.

This is why presliced English muffins are so much easier. The decisions have already been made and acted upon. The only thing that can offend a presliced English muffin is the person whose eating habits reveal her misguided belief that the bottom half is inferior to the top half. The truth is, both halves are equal. Different, yes, but equal by every relevant criterion. Moreover, there is no top and bottom to an English muffin. It's strictly a matter of perspective.

I left the package of English muffins unopened on the table and turned my attention to preparing the tuna fish. The first step was to open the two cans. I left the ragged-edged lids resting upon the tuna meat. I ran tap water over the cans. The lids kept the meat from escaping and the water washed it clean. Then I used the tines of a fork and jimmied the lids free from the cans.

I took a mixing bowl from the cupboard, a large one so nothing would spill when I flaked the tuna and blended in the mayonnaise. I took one tuna can and swiftly turned it upside down and snapped it against the rim of the bowl. The tuna meat fell into the bowl in one chunk leaving the can empty except for a few negligible freckles of tuna which remained behind. Perhaps I became overconfident and thus careless with the second can. There's no point in blaming myself, but something went wrong.

When I examined the second can after snapping it sharply against the mixing bowl's rim, it was not empty. A large chunk of white tuna meat, one-fifth to one-fourth the original contents of the can, sat lodged against the tin perimeter. Was that its intent? Perhaps that chunk of tuna was determined to escape consumption and clung for dear life to an oily toe-hold in the can. Yes. It is likely that tuna fish is terrified of human jaws and the chunk that resisted the gravitational pull toward the mixing bowl was now breathing a sigh of relief. Under such circumstances the only humane thing to do would be to spare it.

On the other hand, that chunk of tuna might have remained behind not deliberately but accidentally. Perhaps right now it was desperately wishing it could be reunited with its wombmates in the mixing bowl. Who knows?

Maybe there are people sensitive enough to discern what it is a chunk of tuna wants. Unfortunately I am not one of them. I can only second guess and do the best I can not to inflict pain. I can never be certain in matters like these.

With a fork, I removed the lonely chunk of tuna from the can. In any case it should be with the tuna fish with which it was originally packed. I placed it in the mixing bowl and with a different fork, share the work that none should be idle, I slowly stirred the fish. Of course I couldn't possibly eat from the bowl now since the action of that special chunk may have signified its resistance to death between human teeth. I stirred until all the fish was flaked and blended. I held the mixing bowl over the brown paper garbage bag and with a clean fork scraped the fish from the bowl into the bag.

I would not need to use the mayonnaise now. At least I was thankful for that. I put the two jars of mayonnaise into the refrigerator, one on top of the other, careful to put the one which had previously been on the bottom on the top.

The raisins which I had bought for dessert would now be my first course. The two boxes of raisins stood on the table an inch apart awaiting their fate. The raisin maids faced each other squarely but did not touch. Perhaps they would like to touch each other before I consumed their contents and disposed of them. I took one box in each hand and brought the two boxes together. The mouths of the raisin maids were now pressing together as were their breasts and bodies. Gently, almost imperceptibly, I rubbed the two boxes together. The raisin maids were making love. They had perfect privacy for this by grace of certain laws of geometry which always grant privacy to any two touching surfaces.

On the other hand they might not be making love at all. The two raisin maids might be nauseated, sick to their stomachs because I had thrown their bodies into contact, one against the other. I separated them instantly. How could I apologize? Was an apology in order? Perhaps it was my separating them, terminating their embrace which was the act that warranted an apology. I had no way of knowing how they wanted to spend their last moments on this earth.

But their time had come. They had been together and apart and I could do no more for them. I must work very quickly. I emptied their contents. Two boxes full of raisins sat in a pile on the table. Arbitrarily (how else could I choose?) I selected one of the empty boxes and placed it in a drawer. The raisin maid would no doubt be frightened alone in that drawer but less frightened than she would be watching her sister's execution.

I unfolded the box which would go first, changing it from a three-dimensional entity to a sheet of cardboard by untucking tabs and slipping my fingernail between glued edges. The raisin maid was now surrounded by a large field predominantly red. I took her feet in my left hand, her head in my right hand with my thumb covering her eyes. Like the agents of the Grand Inquisitor who manifest whatever grains of kindness resided in their evil hearts by strangling their victims before burning them on their stakes, I creased the cardboard rapidly, in one deft motion, right above my thumb, between the head and shoulders of the raisin maid, and broke her neck.

I placed the corpse with its cardboard bier in the mixing bowl and removed the second raisin maid from her death row drawer. I executed her in the same way and placed her body in the mixing bowl. I lit the two bodies on fire. As they burned I sat down to prepare the raisins for their fate.

I began to sort the raisins into groups of twelve. This allows for maximum flexibility within each group. The raisins within each group can form couples, quadruples, sextets, or even triplets if that's a stable form for them, or they can remain in twelves. Grouping by twelves greatly reduced the chances of individual members being left out.

I counted out six groups of twelve and arranged them equidistantly on the table. What remained was a group of which looked the size of the others and might, I hoped, contain exactly twelve members. I counted thirteen. Thirteen raisins. My worst fear had been realized. Not that I'm superstitious. The number thirteen holds no mystical significance for me. This was entirely a practical and specific misfortune, but a dreadful misfortune nevertheless. Thirteen raisins meant a group of twelve with one raisin left over. All in all there were seven groups of twelve and one lone raisin with no place to go. I took the thirteenth raisin in my hand.

I was responsible. The thirteenth raisin had done nothing to justify being left out so cruelly. It was entirely my poor planning. What I should have done when it came to the last group was to count by sight instead of pointing and verbalizing each number. Had I counted silently no raisin would have known who the thirteenth was. The raisins in a group of thirteen surrounded by six groups of twelve would of course know they belonged to an odd group. But the onus would be shared by the entire group and the situation could not, by the farthest stretch of imagination, be considered tragic.

But stupidly I had counted out loud. Everyone knew who the thirteenth raisin was, the raisin who didn't fit.

I held the lone raisin in my hand and explained quietly that this lone raisin was special, that it was in fact the queen over seven groups of twelve raisins. It was queen over eighty-four subjects and as queen it must stand alone. The queen raisin would be the first to enter my mouth and be consumed by me. It must be brave and set the example for its eighty-four subjects. Of course the queen would be brave.

But I couldn't do it. I knew my explanation was a lie. And what makes me think raisins are gullible? A shoddy lie would not suffice to make the thirteenth raisin feel anything less than painful isolation. And even if the raisin had believed my story, there is no telling whether or not it would want to be queen. It might be that raisins despise the idea of being queens or kings as much as humans despise the idea of being subjects.

There was no recourse. I had taken two perfectly good boxes of raisins and prepared them for consumption incorrectly. I placed the thirteenth raisin in the center of the table surrounded by the seven groups. I leaned over the table and with my hands and arms pushed the seven groups, simultaneously, toward the centered raisin until it was thoroughly immersed in a sea of its eighty-four siblings. With my hand I shovelled them all into the garbage.

Once again there was nothing left to eat but English muffins. I didn't mind. English muffins make a very pleasant meal.

S. Evyn Rubin

CATS, DOGS AND COCKROACHES

A cat Being cured of Hairballs, through A television Ministry

place your right paw on the screen

Nicole Hollander

CAT
BRAIN TEASER

1. Who is your owner?

A.   B.   C.   D.

2. Which of the following is inedible?

A.   B. Dry Bits   C.   D.

3. Name the scratchpost

A.   B   C.   D.

4. What happened to your little mouse-toy?

A   B.   C.   D.

Under couch   Behind bookcase   Turned into a ghost

I don't know and what's the difference?

R. Chast

ROZ CHAST

It Does Happen To A Dog

For mere devotion paid to me
    My canny dog is getting
The proper food, a place to sleep,
    And lots of love and petting.

He's not so dumb, this animal
    I spend my time and dough on.
I'd like that deal myself — good food,
    A place to sleep . . . and so on.

IRENE WARSAW

What the Dogs Have Taught Me

Daily Routine
The day is divided into two important sections. *Mealtime.* And *everything else.*

I. Mealtime

1. Just because there does not seem to be anything *visible* around to eat certainly does not mean there is *nothing* around to eat. The act of staring at the underside of a table or chair on which someone else is eating sets in motion a chain of events that eventually results in food.
2. It goes without saying that you should carefully check the lower third of *any* space for edibles. Mouth-sized things which cannot be identified by sight or smell are considered gum.
3. When you actually receive a meal, submerge your head into it as you would a shower. *Never, ever* look up again until a minimum of at least fifteen minutes after the obvious food is gone. This is important. Just because your dish is empty does not mean that it is time to stop eating.
4. Remember that *all* food is potentially yours up until the time that it is actually swallowed by another. The lengthy path a piece of food will take from a plate to a mouth via a hand is as good a time as any to stake your claim to it.

5. When it comes to selecting an appropriate beverage, location and packaging mean *nothing*. There are *absolutely no exceptions* to this rule.
6. If you really see something you want, and all your other attempts at getting it have failed, it is only right to grovel shamelessly. As a second tactic, stare intently at the object of your desire, allowing long gelatinous drools to leak like icicles from your lower lip.

II. *Everything Else*

1. There are really only two important facial expressions to bother with: *complete overwhelming joy* and *nothing at all*.
2. Any time that is not meal time is potentially nap time. The best time to take a nap is when you hear your name being called repeatedly. The best location for a nap is dead center of any street or driveway. The most relaxing position is on your side, all four limbs parallel.
3. The most practical way to get dry is to shake violently near a fully clothed person. A second effective method is to stand on a light-colored piece of furniture.
4. *Personal Security*
    A. At the first hint of any irregular noise, run from room to room yelling loudly. If someone actually comes into the house, rush over to them whether you know them or not. Then kiss them so violently that they lose their balance or have to force you away physically.
    B. The greatest unacknowledged threat to life as we have come to know it is squirrels. No matter what you must do, make sure there are none in your yard.
5. *Recreation and Leisure*
    A. *Ball:* There are two equally amusing sets of rules you will want to know:
        a. *The common form,* in which you receive a thrown ball and return it.
        b. *The preferred form,* in which you receive a thrown ball and eat it.
    B. *Car:* As you know, any open car door is an invitation to get in. Once inside, your only goal is to try to get out.
6. *Health*
    A. In the event of a trip to the doctor, always be on your guard. If you are vaccinated, urinate on the physician.

Since I have taken to sleeping under the bed, I have come to know tranquillity I never imagined possible.

You never really know when it might be cookie time. And that's what the dogs have taught me.

MERRILL MARKOE

'FESSOR FELINE'S *Cat School*

LESSON #3: COMPANY!

① DOORBELL RINGS. HIDE FOR A LONG TIME.

② COME OUT.

③ DISCOVER THE CAT HATER. BOTHER INCESSANTLY.

TAP TAP

④ FIND FOCAL POINT OF ROOM.

⑤ LICK ANUS.

IMPORTANT GUEST

MORE IMPORTANT GUESTS ←

⑥ MAKE DISTRACTING SCRATCHING NOISES IN OTHER ROOM.

SCRATCH

RRRIP

SHRED

⑦ GET YELLED AT.

PRICELESS HEIRLOOM →

⑧ MAKE CRASHING SOUND

CRASH

⑨ HIDE.

©1988 Jennifer Berman

JENNIFER BERMAN

NICOLE HOLLANDER

A Little Misunderstanding

As Corrine Bender lifted the garage door, she became aware of the odor. Warily she stepped into the darkened garage, but it was apparently empty. She stopped near a pile of newspapers she was saving for the recycling center. At her feet was a scattering of cigarette butts. The garage smelled of the smoke.

"That does it," she exclaimed. Corrine marched inside and called the police.

For three weeks it had been evident that neighborhood teenagers had been using her garage and back yard as a meeting place while she was gone. It had started shortly after she took a part-time job at the bank. Summer vacation had left a few of the neighborhood children with nothing to do.

"They have done no damage," she told the desk sergeant on the phone, "but they are trespassing and I am concerned about a fire; today the cigarette butts were dangerously close to some papers in the garage." At least they were regular cigarettes.

"Technically they are breaking the law," the sergeant replied. "Since you say you've already tried to talk to them and had no success, I'll send someone out."

Corrine sighed as she hung up. She was not totally comfortable with her decision. There had to be a better way to deal with the situation.

Morton Deebs was also uncomfortable. When you drove a van that carried a four-foot plastic cockroach on the roof, people stared. Not that he blamed them. Would he have been less uncomfortable had the cockroach not been positioned upon its back, its incompliant legs reaching unceremoniously for the sky? It was really quite undignified, thought Morton, as he pulled into a quiet cul de sac. Had he owned Conrad Exterminators, the roach would be the first thing to go. He sensed that clients did not care to advertise to the neighbors that they had a need for his services, and the cockroach certainly announced quite plainly the purpose of his visit.

Morton Deebs parked on the corner, back away from the houses. The order sheet indicated that 709 Aspen Avenue was in need of roach ridding. 709 Aspen was a tidy white cottage with green shutters. Morton approved; he was, himself, a very tidy man.

The order indicated that he should arrive no sooner than two o'clock and it was only one. He left the equipment in the van. No use hauling it to the door if no one was home. He walked past the neatly trimmed hedge and rang the bell. The lady of the house answered.

"Oh! Come right in," said the pleasant looking woman who answered the door. "Thank you so much for coming."

"How do you do? I'm Morton Deebs. May I have your name? It seems to have been left off my order sheet."

"Of course. I'm Corrine Bender."

Morton copied the name carefully. "I understand you have a problem."

"I do, indeed." Corrine ushered the man into the living room. "I want you to understand that they haven't done any real damage yet . . ."

"But you wouldn't want to wait until that happens, would you? Better to deal with it now."

"Of course. And they deserve to be punished," stated Corrine firmly.

"Punished?"

"That's not my only motive for calling you here, though. I'm doing this for their own good, even though they won't realize it." Corrine was still concerned about neighbor reaction to her call to the police.

"You know, I didn't just panic and call you the first thing. I tried to deal with the problem directly myself."

"Well, Mrs. Bender, that's most commendable. But most people find this sort of situation requires the services of a professional."

"Oh, really? I was naive. I tried talking to them."

Morton Deebs had been in Post Control for three years. In that time, he had heard of people stepping on cockroaches, spraying them with aerosol canisters, poisoning them, trapping them in sticky little boxes, and moving away from them by selling the family home. Morton Deebs had never met anyone who had tried talking to them.

"I tried," continued Corrine, "to be pleasant to them, to reason with them."

"How . . . how did they react?" stammered Morton Deebs.

"It had no effect whatsoever. They continued pestering me."

At this point, Morton felt he had two choices. He could excuse himself and leave. Or he could do his job as quickly as possible. And leave. The main thing was to leave, because this lady was a little strange. But Morton, being a tidy man, did not like leaving things undone. He stood resolutely.

"Now that I'm here, you won't have to worry about a thing. I'll see that they never bother you again. Tell me where you've noticed them."

"In the back yard and the garage," replied Corrine. She liked the no-nonsense attitude of this man. He would take care of everything.

"Okay, but I'm going to check out the house as well."

"Oh," Corrine's hand flew to her mouth. "I'm sure they haven't come into the house."

But Corrine glanced around. The thought made her quite uncomfortable.

"You would be surprised and shocked, Mrs. Bender, at the places they find to hide." With the authority of a man who is going to get the job done, Morton headed for the kitchen.

"Wait!" Corrine for a moment was concerned about his manner. She wanted the problem dealt with, but would he be tactful or would he alienate her from the neighbors?

"Perhaps it's not necessary for you to see them today. Actually, I was hoping that seeing your car parked out front would throw a scare into them."

Morton Deebs stopped so suddenly that Mrs. Bender nearly collided with him. As it was, he had to step back to avoid standing nose to nose with the woman. He had never before met anyone who was crazy. A more curious man would have paused and questioned. A witty man would have quipped, "Perhaps I could play a flute and we could lead them all out to the front yard for a good look."

But Morton was neither a curious man nor a witty one. The lady had bats in her belfry, but she also had cockroaches in her garage—and probably in her kitchen too, if Morton Deebs knew his cockroaches.

"I'll just take a moment," said Morton as he turned and kneeled on the kitchen floor and opened the doors of the cupboard under Corrine's sink. He ducked his head in, pulled out a tiny flashlight, and made a quick search.

Had Mr. Deebs been looking, he would have seen Corrine's jaw drop noticeably, her eyes widen, and her hand fly to her breast. Of course, Morton did not see these things, his head being under the sink in a cupboard. And it was just this circumstance which caused Corrine's reaction. She had never had a policeman in her cupboard before. She was not expecting one to be there today. Corrine did not like the unexpected. She turned to look at the clock. Her husband, Frank, would not be home for hours. Did one scream under such circumstances? Corrine did not have time to decide what the appropriate behavior was.

"Now," announced Morton Deebs, "I'll check your attic."

"My attic?"

"The attic," lectured Morton, as he strode down the hall, "is a favorite hiding place. They like to hide between the walls, too."

"Wait. I assure you, it is not necessary to search my attic."

Corrine was successful in steering Morton Deebs back to the living room. Morton was losing patience.

"Mrs. Bender, if I am not to be permitted to handle this situation in my own way, then perhaps I'd better leave."

"I think I need to hear more about your methods before we take this any further," said Corrine Bender firmly. This man was not behaving in an appropriate manner at all. And, to her relief, he had just offered to leave, which meant he did not intend to harm her.

"What would you like to know?" asked Morton Deebs.

"I can tell you where they are. What I want to know is what do you intend to do with them when you find them?" asked Corrine Bender.

Morton Deebs took a breath. As if speaking to a very slow child, he replied, "I am going to kill them."

The blood drained from Corrine Bender's face. Her heart pounded loudly in her chest—so loudly that her hands flew to cover her ears. Her eyes snapped open in horror. Get the man out and then get help. But be careful. Don't alarm him. She brought her hands down and smoothed her dress.

"I thought, perhaps, just a warning this time."

"You've already tried that, Mrs. Bender," Morton carefully replied.

"But coming from you a warning would mean so much more to them."

Morton Deebs could not picture himself talking to cockroaches, even to appease a customer. Such behavior did not reflect the dignity with which Morton credited himself.

"Mrs. Bender, I've been in this business for several years and I've never met one you could reason with."

Morton Deebs headed for the door. He had never lost a customer before, and he wasn't sure how he was going to explain this to Mr. Conrad.

"I'm sorry to have wasted your time, but I can't let you hurt them," said Corrine as she walked him to the door.

"It has been," replied Morton Deebs, "a most interesting experience."

As he walked down the sidewalk, he pulled the order sheet from his pocket. He would have to figure out what he was going to write on it; he certainly had not completed the job.

"Oh, dear," whispered Morton Deebs to himself. Instead of visiting 709 Aspen Lane, he had knocked on the wrong door and visited 706 instead. He checked his watch. It was 1:30. He still had time to make the appointment.

As Morton Deebs was ringing the bell at 709, Corrine Bender was standing open-mouthed in her front yard staring at an absurd van parked a short distance away. Atop the vehicle was a very large, dead, four-foot cockroach. There was no patrol car in sight.

Moments later, however, one pulled up at 706 Aspen Lane. The neighborhood seemed, to the police officer in the driver's seat, to be pleasant and quiet, except for the woman sitting on the lawn, laughing uncontrollably as tears rolled down her face. She was, obviously, hysterical.

MARCIA FRIGAARD STEIL

GOD, JESUS CHRIST, THE POPE & THE ONE TRUE ANSWER

ALL THINGS
by LYNDA BARRY © 1990

DEAR GOD I AM HEARTILY SORRY FOR HAVING BEEN RANKING ON YOU. IT'S JUST THAT MY LIFE TURNED SO CRUDDY AND ALSO WE'VE BEEN STUDYING THE CRUDDINESS OF THE WORLD IN ALL CLASSES EXCEPT MATH SO I WAS RIDING ON A BUMMER.

BUT THEN YOU SHOWED ME THE BEAUTY OF LIFE BY GIVING ME DAVID AND I HAD SUCH A FUN TIME WITH HIM AT SUE AKERS PARTY THANK YOU SO MUCH. ABOUT THE CRUDDINESS OF THE WORLD THOUGH, I STILL DON'T GET YOUR MYSTERIOUS WAYS. IN LANGUAGE ARTS WE ARE READING THE DIARY OF ANNE FRANK. HAVE YOU READ THIS BOOK?

YA PRAYIN'?

YEAH.

YEAH.

OUR TEACHER SHOWED US PICTURES OF THE PEOPLE IN THAT TIME AND NO ONE IN OUR CLASS COULD EVEN TALK. BUT I GUESS YOU KNOW THIS BECAUSE YOU KNOW ALL THINGS. YOU EVEN KNOW WHAT MY REPORT'S GOING TO SAY AND WHAT'S MY GRADE ON IT, AND NORMALLY I WOULDN'T BUG YOU FOR HELP ON THIS BUT I'M BUSTED FOR IDEAS, SO PLEASE GIVE YOUR ANSWER, AMEN, LOVE, MAYBONNE. P.S. IT'S NOT JUST ME BUT A LOT OF PEOPLE WANT TO KNOW.

I'M SORRY IF IT GETS ON YOUR NERVES, MY IRRITATING QUESTIONS, BUT I THINK YOU'RE SO COOL AND SUPER POWERFUL AND NOT CONCEITED PLUS I HAVE TO WRITE A PAPER ON ANNE FRANK. REMEMBER MY PAPER ON PREDJUDICE WHERE YOU GAVE ME THE ANSWER OF <u>LOVE EACH OTHER</u> AND I GOT AN <u>A</u>? OK. SO I WANT TO WRITE "WHY DID GOD LET THIS HAPPEN?" IT'S DUE THURSDAY.

WANT ME TA HELP?

HUH?

HELP YA.

NAH. THAT'S OK.

LYNDA BARRY

My Older Brother

It was weird, their relationship. I think that it was the main reason Jesus never married. No one was ever as good as Mom. Mom definitely liked him best and this made my brother James and me feel bad. We tried to sell him to the heathen.

But Jesus *was* special. I mean, a lot of people think they're Jesus but Jesus actually was Jesus. We were all proud of him, even if we were also very jealous. No one in our family had ever amounted to much. My Uncle Aaron invented the little hook they use to hang jars on the wall but he never registered it, so he didn't make any money. Other than Uncle Aaron, we were a bunch of nobodies. Then there was Jesus. Even as a little kid, he was the only one of us ever to make the "gifted class." But he dropped out of school early because he didn't see the point, given what he wanted to do eventually.

It's a shame. He could have been a really great philosopher or something.

Jesus was always the most popular. We moved around a lot— Bethlehem, Nazareth, we fled to Egypt, then back to Nazareth—so I guess his talent for making friends in a snap was some psychological means of adapting. Even the older kids looked up to Jesus. He could do amazing things. We'd sit for hours with our fishing rods, trying to catch one measly trout and then Jesus would come strolling along and . . . you know, kazam.

You might accuse Jesus of being a show-off but you never could say he used his connections with God to get wealth or friends.

The other neat thing he could do was bend all his fingers back so they touched his forearm.

When he was seven, James set up a school that claimed to teach people how to do this trick. Of course, he was a big fraud and everyone's mothers barged into our house the next day, demanding their kids' money back.

After Jesus died and one of his disciples—Bartholomew, I think—came by to tell us that he had been resurrected, we had to smile even though it was supposedly a sad time. Good old Jesus, up to his old tricks!

Definitely, there were some good things about being related to Jesus. We got into a lot of theatrical events and other amusements free, and in Nazareth, we were allowed to tie up our livestock on any road.

But there were bad sides. With Jesus around, we could never get any peace and quiet. Wherever the Christs went as a family, people followed, especially lepers. "Jesus get my son a job, Jesus will you introduce me to Ruth of the Wheatfields, Jesus this, Jesus that."

Jesus was the anointed one. He was Jesus Christ! I was just plain Jane Christ. My parents were very understanding. They tried to make each of us feel special.

"Jesus may be better than you," they said, "but you have a delicate touch when it comes to folding and a lovely speaking voice."

PATRICIA MARX

THE BABY JESUS
DISCOVERS
HIS
PENIS

ROSALIND WARREN

Maggie

I was thirty-seven years old and Joe and me had been married eighteen years and I'd never been pregnant though I'd prayed for a baby almost ever' night. Then one day, Mother Mary appeared to me in a vision while I was peelin' potatoes and said, "Margaret," which was strange, 'cause nobody's called me Margaret since Aunt Maggie died and she only called me Margaret so people'd know she wasn't talkin' to herself. But, anyway, Mother Mary said, "Margaret, you will get your fondest wish and have a baby if you will stop shavin' your legs and armpits." Just like that. Then she disappeared right into thin air.

Well, I couldn't hardly believe it, but I did just what she said and didn't shave no more. Joe didn't like it at first, but after a while he kinda got used to it and not mor'n two months later I got pregnant. I was so happy I cried.

Now I'm forty years old and I got this three-year-old kid that's runnin' around askin' me "why" this and "how come" that and "what for" ever'thing. I mean even early in the mornin' he gets out of his crib and comes in my room and stands there stickin' his finger up my nose while I'm trying to sleep and starts sayin', "Mama, why you got two holes in your nose?" I tell you, it's drivin' me crazy.

And Mother Mary never showed her face to me again. I even started shavin' my legs and armpits like I used to, but it didn't do no good.

DONNA DeCLUE

Excerpt from: "Man, Wife and Deity"

All of a sudden, Lillian got religion and started talking about the Goddess. *Thank Goddess!* she would exclaim with heartfelt sentiment, or, when exasperated, *O, Goddess!* For several months, she went through a phase of reading the Bible at night in bed, muttering darkly, *It's the Word of God, alright, every last lie.*

DIANE LEFER

What About The Pope?

The world population appears to be made up mostly of heterosexual people. Pervasive as they are, we can't help but sometimes wonder about them. What *are* they? *Who* are they? And why do they choose the life they do? These are only a few of the mysteries that could begin to unfold if only science would allocate more research funds to these neglected questions. We can only wait, and hope.

One thing I've noticed in particular about straight people—and I've known a lot of them so I think I can talk—is that when they find out you're lesbian, they inevitably ask, sooner or later, this famous question: "Why is it that so *many* lesbians dress like men?"

This is the one they all ask, even the more intelligent or enlightened ones who don't ask the usual list of other inane things.

Well, I have a question for you, Straight People. What I want to know is, why is it that so *many* straight people are so utterly obsessed with this dress-like-men question? If it's so fascinating, why don't *you* dress like men?

And anyway, what do you mean, "dress like men?" Which men? What about all the women who dress like all the men who dress like Barbie? Aren't they, then, "dressing like men" too? What about the Pope? Is the Pope wearing a dress or is he not? Raise your hand if you have EVER seen the Pope wearing slacks. And look, he's a straight person. At least, that's what he would have you believe, what with all his trashing of gay people. (The official stand of the Catholic Church, for those of you who are not Pope-watchers, is "It's *alright* to be gay, but only if you're really sorry and promise never to act on your perverse feelings.")

It isn't hard to understand, if you look at what the man is wearing, why he feels he has to go on and on about it, why he feels he has to go the extra mile to make it *perfectly clear* that he's not gay. Because though you and I know that this is ONLY a STEREOTYPE, you have to realize that *most of the public* thinks that if you're a man, and you wear a dress, especially an elaborate and expensive, brocaded and embroidered *multi-layered* dress with a fey little hat and lots of accessories, it means you're gay. (We don't even know anyone like that, do we girls?)

Well, since he evidently hasn't heard, I'm here to tell the Pope that the latest information gradually seeping into public awareness is that—good news!—(you'll be so relieved) it doesn't mean that you're gay, it only means that you're a transvestite. And did you know, Mr. Pope, that *most* (87% according to a poll by Field & Stream) of all transvestites are STRAIGHT?

Yes, it's true. And as self-appointed spokesgoddess for the lesbian community on Catholicism, I want to say, Mr. Pope, that we all *know* you're a transvestite, and it's *O-KAY!* Really. *We're not prejudiced.* Some of our best friends are transvestites.

Why, all over the globe, husbands are secretly dressing up in their wives' underwear and enjoying every minute of it. I'm not, however, implying that the Pope does that. We all know he doesn't have a wife, for one thing. And for another thing I would never be so disrespectful as to speculate on what kind of underwear he does wear. It doesn't even matter to me. I have other things to think about, believe me. Like what kind of underwear am *I* going to wear tomorrow, since I haven't done my laundry in twelve days.

And Mr. Pope, if you are gay, well we don't know that because that's your private life and you choose not to be as public with that as you are with your transvesticism. At least if we don't count the fact that the entire world knows that you're living with a lot of other men. I for one don't sit around wondering if the Pope has a boyfriend.

I just happen to think it's noteworthy that when it comes to the really important things, like God, and the Supreme Court, suddenly the boys get to wear dresses. That's all.

But as long as I'm talking about all this, I might as well take the opportunity to answer, once and for all, the question that plagues so *many* straight people — for the benefit of the 3.5 million of them who are probably reading this book.

Okay! Here it is! The moment of Truth you've all been waiting for! The ANSWER — to one of the Mysteries of the Universe!!

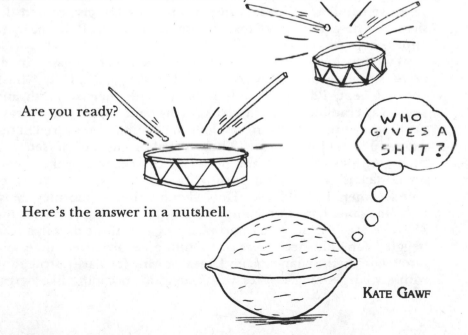

Are you ready?

WHO GIVES A SHIT?

Here's the answer in a nutshell.

Kate Gawf

Confession

Dear Father Collins:

I'm not sure exactly how to start, but there are times in life when philosophical rumination must give way to action. So, I sit down at my typewriter today and attempt to unravel the ribbon of truth knotted by years of neglect and silence. I pray that it makes a silken bow in your lap.

It's been over fifteen years since I saw you last. I've always felt guilty about the way we parted. You were my teacher, my confessor, but especially my friend. Cursing and throwing my Holy Missal at you in church was really uncalled for. I wish to make amends for such *jejune* behavior. More than an apology, however, I wish to explain and clarify my actions, clear the air between us.

I never missed a Mass you were offering, a retreat you were conducting, a sermon you were delivering. I volunteered to help the Sisters feed the hungry, to grade your examination papers, to bake fresh bread for the rectory, even to change the dead flowers on the altar so I could stand in the same place you did when you were suffused with the Eternal. I suppose you thought I was a holy girl, a child gifted with a vocation to serve God, a fledgling saint. Not true. Oh, not true at all!

For I was madly in love with you, irredeemably smitten and enthralled with you. Your firm compassionate voice, your eyes the color of warm caramel, the heady scent of myrrh and beeswax that clung to your robes, all drove me wild. And your hands! Your fine sensitive hands that blessed, forgave, fed the hungry, healed the sick, and held the Holy Host. Those same hands that began to appear in my dreams.

I was seventeen. Strange hormones were wrecking havoc in my body, storming the ramparts of my Temple of the Holy Ghost. When I slept, I'd feel your holy hands with their strength and sensitivity cradling my head, stroking my hair, cupping my breast, probing my Inner Sanctum. Yes, I blush to admit, you starred in the erotic cinema of my dreams. Their sexual beauty was infused with such gorgeous sensuality and powerful innocence that these nocturnal fantasies could not possibly be sinful. I was disturbed, of course, when I would take Holy Communion at morning Mass from the same hands which had caressed my aching loins just the night before. Tormented, I started fasting two, three days in a row, begging for guidance. I began spending all my recess time and lunch hour in the chapel on my knees, praying for clarity, struggling with my burgeoning lust for you which was spreading like heresy through my entire endocrine system. I didn't know right from wrong, good from evil, the holy from the profane. Was it God or was it Satan that compelled these erotic urges on me?

It all came to a head that fateful Saturday. I had finally realized it was essential to speak with you directly, to confess my dreams and purge myself of sin. I waited until your confessional booth was free. "Bless me Father, for I have sinned. It's been a month since my last confession."

"Yes, my child," you said.

"Father, I have had impure thoughts . . . I . . . that is to say, umh . . .," I hesitated. Cold sweat sailed down my armpits.

"Yes, my daughter? Tell me what kind of impure thoughts have been troubling you. God is merciful," you said.

"Well, damn it, Father, I love you!" and out gushed all my lust, anxieties, and sinful imaginings—how I wanted you and your holy hands, how your lectures on reproduction in biology class were driving me into a whirlwind of lechery, how I craved to worship on my knees at the Temple of your Manhood hidden under your holy robes. "Father, I know I'm a blasphemous strumpet, but I want you, I need you so much, even it if means going to hell! What shall we do about this?"

And then you committed the most heinous sin. You laughed! Yes, you laughed at me and said, "My child, you have much too much of a fevered imagination. I suggest you take a cold shower and have the nurse check your temperature. Say five Hail Marys and three Our Fathers. *Te absolvo.*"

I was prepared for punishment and penance, I was prepared for scorn and derision, but I was not prepared for patronage and dismissal. Stung by humiliation, I leapt out of the booth, jerked aside the confessional curtain, and hurled my prayerbook at you. Choked with rage, I screamed that God would punish you. I fled down the aisle, leaving behind both the Church and my faith in God's goodness.

I savagely ended my virginity with the first divinity student I could find. I quit going to Mass, got a job at Planned Parenthood, started on the pill, and embarked on a ferocious period of religious promiscuity. I hung around ecclesiastical book stores and Newman Clubs; there were always plenty of boys eager to have a more tangible divine experience. I was flushed with the heady wine of sacrilege as I haunted devotional article stores, demanding the most erotic holy cards, the most provocative plastic Jesuses. I always thought of you.

Of course, there's been a lot of holy water under the bridge since then. I am chagrined as I reflect on those days. I am writing to you to ask you forgiveness for my adolescent defiance of so long ago. I was very young and felt things perhaps too intensely. I still have the utmost admiration for you and would like us to be friends.

I enclose a recent photograph. You can see I am in glowing health, have tried to restore my body as a Temple for the Holy Ghost, and my breasts are 100% natural, no silicone. I would love to invite you to dinner at my apartment. My phone number is on the back of the photo.

I remember your favorite Beatitude was, "Blessed are the peacemakers, for they shall inherit the Kingdom of Heaven." Since I know your place in heaven has already been secured, I hope you will find it in your heart to forgive my transgressions of so long ago and allow me to give you the piece on earth you so richly deserve.

Pax,

Mary ♡

ALEXANDRA MORGAN

The One True Answer

Stuff your face with chocolate —
That's the only way,
Stuff your face with chocolate —
Till the world goes away
So stuff your face with chocolate
Come what may, just
STUFF YOUR FACE WITH CHOCOLATE
AND LIE IN BED ALL DAY.
Who cares about revolution?
Or that the world may end by noon —
Us languorous chocoholics
Are not responsible for its ruin.

LORRAINE SCHEIN

PERIOD PIECES

THE CHOSEN FAMILY

NOREEN STEVENS

Miss Den'orea

The bloody bitch

She visits me once a month
To remind me of my gender

She gives me a pain

EVELYN ROEHL

NICOLE HOLLANDER

A Period Is Just the Beginning of a Life Long Sentence

When we were 10 and our teacher passed out the nifty little booklets about becoming a woman (you know, when the boys had to go play baseball), getting a period seemed like it would be the most elegant experience imaginable. Even when that fantasy passed, menstruation was still a great way to get out of gym class or "gross out" your friends at slumber parties.

Now, more than 20 years after we learned that not all napkins belong on the dinner table, some of us are getting fed up with this whole business of menstrual periods. Haven't we suffered enough? The stresses of ebbing and waning estrogen levels are an enormous drain on the mature womanpower of this nation. Not to mention the debilitating sense of helplessness we feel in the face of rising tampon costs.

The Non-Menstrual Sabbatical

Let's face it—the only sure way to escape the stress of the menstrual cycle is to take a vacation from the whole business. If there were any justice in this world, women would receive time off for good behavior—perhaps Non-Menstrual Sabbaticals of a year or more, having nothing to do with pregnancy or menopause. The coveted sabbaticals, sponsored by a publicly-funded foundation, would be awarded annually to a thousand women over thirty years of age who had a demonstrated need to be free of monthly distress. Here's a sample application:

APPLICATION FOR PERIOD OF TIME WITHOUT PERIODS
    Name: Polly Progesteron
    Occupation: Copywriter, Midol Company
    Number of years menstruating: 21
    Pairs of underwear ruined: 8
    Romances seriously threatened by violent mood changes: 3
    Cumulative cost of sanitary products: $1500
    In several sentences, describe your most embarrassing moment related to menstruation: It was at a party. I was wearing a new pair of white flannel trousers. I was having a great time, when suddenly one of my female friends took me aside and whispered in my ear. Do I have to go on? It's a painful memory.
    In 150 words or less, tell us how you feel about getting your period: Like, I can't stand it! First, I feel yucky for days. I bloat up and

I snap at everybody around me. I feel that way for about six days before, and then, when I get it, it's a pain too. You know what I mean? It seems that almost half my month is taken up waiting to get it and then getting it.

If awarded our Sabbatical Fellowship, how would you use it to the best advantage? (250 words or less, please). Since I think I am a fairly productive person as it is, I estimate that the eleven days I would gain each month by not worrying about my period would free me up to help man- and womankind. Among the projects I am considering for my non-menstruating hiatus are: establishing peace in the Middle East, finding a cure for cancer, inventing a diaphragm for men and opening the first outerspace PMS clinic on the Space Shuttle.

Recommendations: Please list three people who could tell the foundation about how menstruation has affected you over the years.

Name	Relationship
Mrs. Jones	High School Phys. Ed Teacher
Luna Menarche	Best Friend
Ronald Cramp	Ex-husband

Or maybe the non-menstruating sabbaticals wouldn't have to be administered by application at all. Perhaps they could follow the model of the MacArthur Fellowships, the "genius" awards of several hundred thousand dollars dished out annually to unsuspecting artists and scientists by a Chicago foundation.

Imagine it. You come home dead tired from the office one day to find a fancy-looking envelope with a return address, "The Non-Menstrual Sabbatical Fellowship Year." You're about to toss it out, thinking it's a fund-raising drive or a new advertising gimmick for yet another shockingly toxic tampon that will keep lawyers busy for the next few years. But you're intrigued by seeing the word "Menstrual" in bold type. Kicking off your shoes, you slump on the sofa and open the missive. Here's what you read:

Dear Polly,

Congratulations! You have been nominated by a panel of your peers to receive a year-long Non-Menstrual Sabbatical. The award means that you will be free of any uterine complications for twelve months. We are hopeful that a year's respite from such nonsense will free you to accomplish any important task you might have been planning.

Please understand that, unlike so many other products related to menstruation, our sabbatical fellowship comes with no strings attached. However, if, at the end of your experience you would like to contribute a personal essay to our foundation journal, "Empty

Uterus, Busy Mind," we would be most grateful.

We will be expecting to hear from you at your earliest convenience concerning the administration of your award.

Cordially yours,

Margaret Sans Menses,
Co-Chairperson

Alas, the non-menstrual sabbatical is still only in the fantasy stage. But don't despair. With test tube babies already here, can test tube periods be far behind?

CATHY CRIMMINS

NICOLE HOLLANDER

PROCREATION

CLAIRE BRETECHER

excerpt from:

If Men Could Become Pregnant

Men would still be men—with swollen bellies, that instead of carrying excess by-products of malt, hops and water in barrel-shape, would carry something useful: miniature people.

There would be much swaggering around with these bloated bellies. Men would pat each other on the bellies and say things like, "How's it goin', buddy?" and "Wasn't Charlie great in the delivery room last weekend? Man, he was in top form. Did you see that breathing? I'd like to see a play-by-play!"

Trophies would be awarded by Lamaze for best teams of breathers. Purple hearts would be given to those men who went through unmedicated births.

There would be macho movies about childbirth. Clint Eastwood would clench his teeth, squint and say, "Make my day," while pushing; Sylvester Stallone would grunt and sweat profusely while going through a contraction. A movie called *Deliverance* would have a whole new meaning.

MARY GRABAR

NICOLE HOLLANDER

Sue Wanted To Have the Second Baby At Home

"Sue wanted to have the second baby at home but the doctor was very strong against it—her first labor had gone thirty-six hours. Anyway, so she was going to have it at the hospital. But it ended up that she was visiting Maryann, in the kitchen drinking tea, and the water broke and twenty minutes later the baby came. Maryann delivered it. Of course they never would have planned it like that. I mean if Sue was going to have it at home she would have prepared things, found a doctor. Just think, in seventh grade Maryann and Sue used to go shoplifting together, and now this."

ELLEN GRUBER GARVEY

KATE GAWF

Labor

My friend Hope said everyone was lying to us. Or at least not telling us the truth. We were eight months pregnant and not one woman who had had a baby would tell us what it was really like.

"I'll tell you," Judy said at the party. "You know when you've just dropped acid and you are starting to come on to it and you can't do anything about it?"

"Yeah," I said, "that's my least favorite feeling in the world."

"Well," she said, "that's what giving birth is like."

Let me tell you, labor is better than having your heart broken, better than being in a car crash, better than really bad stomach flu, but worse than average stomach flu, better than being panic-stricken about money, and better than having the cat run away. But labor is worse than eating lunch, worse than the meanest thing your mother says on the telephone, worse than ripping two pairs of pantyhose in a row, worse than stage fright, worse than wondering if there is a god. In terms of physical pain it is worse than slamming your finger in the car door because it lasts considerably longer. Drugs help, as indeed does being the center of attention. Nothing else helps, despite what you have been taught. Breathing does not help. Imagining your joy at the birth of a tiny baby does not help. Being rude to people helps a bit, complaining helps more, yelling Jesus Jesus Jesus also helps if you are that sort of person. A glass of water helps only because you get to demand it. When Hope went into labor and hit transition she yelled at her midwife: "What are my options?" "You don't have any options," said the midwife. Hope said that helped.

MIRIAM SAGAN

PLAYMATE

CLAIRE BRETECHER

MORE FEMALE BODY YUCKS

"Oh don't mind that. It's just my biological clock."

A.J. Toos

Femina
a commercial message

Has this ever happened to you? One kiss that leads to another, and before you know it, you're in bed with him, and you're perspiring. Or worse. Sound familiar?

Before he finds out that your body has an odor all its own, use FEMINA, the all-over-and-under-inside-and-out body deodorant just for us women.

FEMINA not only stops embarrassing perspiration, it tracks down all those harsh, unpleasant odors, wherever they hide and mingle, and it kills them— dead.

In laboratory tests, FEMINA's fifteen active ingredients have been proven 97% effective— and mostly safe. The makers of FEMINA guarantee it will keep you dry and odor free in the stickiest of situations, or your money back. That's a promise.

Look, let's be honest: if you're a woman, you're going to smell, and you shouldn't, and he *knows* you shouldn't.

So unless you're only looking for a one-night stand, get FEMINA. And all the two of you will smell—is him.

JULIA WILLIS

PEG

NORMAL AND ALL, but after twenty-five years OF marriage, HAS **NEVER FARTED** in front of husband.

MARY LAWTON

The Yearly Exam

It's that season again. No, I don't mean summer, it is time; once again, for a visit to the gynecologist. Perhaps some of you understand why getting my annual pap smear is not the most joyful of occasions for me. Just as I sincerely feel that men ought to be the ones who get pregnant and go through labor, I also feel they should be the ones who lie on the table on their backs each year, heels high in cold metal stirrups, a sheet covering the top of them and breezes blowing over the exposed lower portions. (For men who do not know: the sheet also acts as a screen so that you cannot see what the doctor is doing down there.) It is an unusual feeling in the best of circumstances. Lights shine so brightly you feel the heat; the doctor mumbles. He or she takes out a speculum which is either cold (wow!) or warmed, either dry (ouch!) or lubricated. Hopefully, since you cannot see, the doctor will describe what he or she is doing. Hopefully, a male intern will not say (as one did) when he is about to insert the speculum: "Here I come."

The speculum has a nasty metallic sound when it opens, but that is nothing compared to the sound it makes closing, like thin metal scissors coming together, "Oh please," I pray, "do not take skin." Once the inner skin has been scraped and I *do feel* it (contrary to the opinion of one doctor who assured me that women had no sensory nerves there), the speculum is removed, and the doctor puts on the rubber glove. It is an awkward feeling to have some straight woman or man poking their fingers deep inside you, asking if anything hurts. By then you have been so violated the breast exam is nothing. I do notice they never look you in the eye while doing it. (I do wish my nipples wouldn't go hard no matter who is touching them.)

I usually tell doctors that I am a lesbian. It is not a form of masochism on my part to come out to a possibly prejudiced and almost-never-comfortable-about-the-issue-of-lesbians *person*. It is to avoid being told I have miscarried when I have bled too hard or avoid being told that I must have tried to abort myself if I am hemorrhaging, and it is to avoid being force-fed birth control. I watch their reaction carefully. Usually I get a blank look and a clinical statement that they are not prejudiced. I get the distinct feeling they wish I were not one of their patients.

I do not encounter these reactions in neighborhood women's clinics. In these clinics one encounters women, both straight and gay, who truly seem to love their work. They talk to you, warm and lubricate the speculum, do their best to educate you further on sexuality and the ways your body operates. I do think they get a little carried away when they bring in the mirror so I can look at my cervix, or call in others to look at my cervix. Rather than celebrate my womanhood, at that point I would simply prefer they removed the speculum as soon as possible. They do look at me while giving a breast exam, say, "Gee, I don't know what this is," and soon everyone is feeling my breasts — but I'm open to it. A second opinion is much preferable to a mammogram, which is rather akin to having your boobs squashed in a waffle iron.

This year I'm more at ease. There are gay and lesbian doctors out there and I have one. My yearly pap and exam are still nothing to celebrate, but at least they are nothing to dread. In a caring setting I can ask the embarrassing and hopelessly naive questions I need to ask. I prefer private physicians because of the dignity and privacy of the setting; a woman's clinic is my second choice. I do remember one hospital clinic where I was given a prescription to fill. I went downstairs to the crowded hospital pharmacy, handed in my prescription and sat down with the other patients. A woman from behind the counter shouted, "Sausser, what clinic did you get this from?" I tried to say quietly, "The fourth floor clinic." Then she said, "What?" and everyone was staring at me. After attempting to say it quietly once more I gave up and shouted, "The V.D. Clinic!" So much for privacy.

GAIL SAUSSER

NOREEN STEVENS

A Tuesday Dilemma

Dr. Zizmor promises
a beautiful clear skin
to every woman
riding in this car,
and *The New York Times* reports
that cynics die
much earlier by far
than true believers.

EDITH GROSSMAN

Small Felonies

The strange events began one afternoon a number of years ago when Hester Jacobs answered the doorbell of her New York apartment and found her sister-in-law, Yetta, standing in the hallway, weeping and wailing. Hester pulled Yetta inside, slammed the door shut, and yelled "Omigod, what happened?"

"I just came from the doctor," Yetta moaned. "After the news he gave me, I think I'm going to kill myself."

"*Vey es mir,* is it cancer?"

"No, it's worse."

"What could be worse?"

"The doctor told me I'm three months pregnant."

"Pregnant?" Hester yelled. "At your age? You're a forty-five year old grandmother! You told me you had gone through the change already."

"I thought I had," Yetta said sadly, "but now I'm changed back."

Hester smacked her forehead with the palm of her hand. "How could this happen to you? Who did this?"

"Your brother Sol, who else?"

"I'd like to kill him," Hester growled through clenched teeth.

"And what good would that do?" Yetta asked plaintively. "Who would support us? No, it's better I should kill myself."

"Stop already with your crazy talk," Hester snapped. "My neighbor next door told me about a doctor, a good one. He takes care of these things."

Yetta's eyes widened in fear. "You mean one of those butchers, an abortionist?"

"You think I would send you to a butcher?" Hester shouted. "This doctor is the finest. Hands of pure gold. He's clean, he's smart, he's very careful to do a good job. I know some high-class ladies who have gone to him; they say he's like a regular saint. And he doesn't charge a lot."

"Who cares about the money?" Yetta said. "Whatever it costs, I'll pay; just so my Solly shouldn't find out!"

Hester put both hands on her hips and sneered, "Solly? What the hell should you care what Solly thinks! You're the sick old grandmother with high blood pressure. Did Sol worry when he got you pregnant? You've got four grown children. At your age you need another baby?

"So, nu, how do I find this doctor?" Yetta asked, with resignation in her voice.

"Don't worry," Hester said, "I'll take care of everything. Just go home and rest so your pressure shouldn't go up. I'll call you as soon as I get an appointment."

Hester made five phone calls through the grapevine before she found the doctor's current address. The next morning at ten she took Yetta to the abortionist's clinic and waited there several hours. Yetta finally came out, white-faced and weak, and Hester drove her home and put her to bed. As Hester got ready to leave, Yetta hugged and kissed her and said, "How can I ever thank you? You saved my life. Just don't tell Sol."

The next five days passed without incident. Hester telephoned Yetta every day, and Yetta said she felt fine. Then, suddenly, on the sixth day, there came a violent pounding on Hester's door. It was her brother, Sol.

"Open up, goddamit, or I'll call the police and tell them you're a criminal, and you'll croak in jail!"

Hester opened the door. Solomon came roaring in, his face blotched red with fury, the veins puffed out on his neck. "What did you do to my Yetta? She won't let me come near her in bed! You murderess! You took her to one of those filthy butchers!"

Hester took a deep breath, crossed her arms over her chest and stood her ground. "Listen, idiot. I did what had to be done. Yetta was ready to kill herself, and *you* would have been the murderer."

"You're a witch with the evil eye," he shouted. "If I had a gun I'd shoot you!"

Hester tossed back her head and laughed. "Hah, such chutzpah you've got! So shoot me, why don't you—and then *you'll* croak in jail! And just remember this: If you shoot me and get your wife far-preggled again, I'll come out of my grave and take you to a doctor who will castrate you! So just keep your mouth shut, keep your pants buttoned up around Yetta, and get the hell out of my house.

You're crazy as a loon!"

With that, she gave him one hard push and slammed the door in his face.

For one year after that scene, Solomon refused to speak to Hester. His wife, Yetta, reported that when anyone mentioned Hester's name, Solomon would say, "Sister? What sister? I have no sister. She's dead." Hester was unfazed, and she and Yetta continued to do their shopping and cooking and to go to movie matinees together as usual.

Two years passed peacefully. Then suddenly one morning Solomon and Yetta appeared together at Hester's door. This time both of them were weeping and wailing. Hester, frightened by all this hysteria, grabbed her hair on both sides of her temples and yelled, "What! What! So tell me what it is!"

Yetta collapsed onto a kitchen chair and covered her face with a handkerchief. Solomon trembled and pressed his two palms together in front of Hester as if he were begging. Hester's back stiffened, her eyes narrowed with suspicion, and in a steely voice she said, "Nu, Sol, so tell me already. I'm waiting."

So whimpered, "It's Yetta. She's had a little accident."

"An accident in the car?"

"No, not in the car, God forbid. A different kind of accident. I don't know how. I tried to be careful. But these things happen."

"What things?"

"Yetta is pregnant."

"Pregnant? And you call that a little *accident*? On *Hitler's* head should fall such an accident!"

"Please, Hester, please! You're my favorite sister. I always loved you best. I'll do anything you say. Yetta is too old and too sick to have another baby. Have pity on us."

Hester raised her eyes to the ceiling and implored, "God, what does this loony man want from my life? God, why do You keep giving children to a man who's an idiot? How in heaven could You wish such bad luck on an innocent baby?"

In a mighty wrath, Hester loomed larger and larger and more stony-eyed; and poor helpless Solomon shrank smaller and smaller under her stare of accusation. He got down on his knees, kissed the hem of Hester's skirt and wailed, "Please, you're our only hope. Call the doctor who took care of Yetta before. Tell him I'll pay him anything—anything!"

With a bitter smirk Hester poked a sharp finger under Sol's nose. "Ahah, Sol! Remember two years ago when I took care of your last so-called 'little accident,' you said if you had a gun you would shoot me? So where is your gun, Sol? Give it to me so I can shoot *you!* The last time you were here, I warned you to keep your pants buttoned when you were with your wife. And did you listen? On you I can only wish an ancient curse: 'You should grow like an onion with your head in the ground and your feet sticking up'!"

Solomon pleaded, "Have pity on us, Hester. Just call that doctor."

But Hester had not yet squeezed her last pound of flesh. "Listen, Sol, you crazy man. Do you know what kind of a doctor it is that you want me to call?"

"Yes, yes, I know. He's an abortionist," Solomon whispered.

Hester adamantly refused to lower her voice. "And do you know that abortion is illegal?"

Sol sobbed. "Yes, but my Yetta said that doctor was a saint. He was like a regular Jesus Christ."

Hester snorted. "Never mind about the Jesus Christ business. I'd just like to remind you that my husband, Nathan, your brother-in-law, is a respectable business man. If anyone found out I took your Yetta for not one, but *two* illegal operations, there would be raised such a stink and a 'schkandahl' that my poor Nathan would be ruined for life."

"Bite your tongue for such a thought," Sol replied, putting his right hand over his heart. "I swear I will go to my grave with my lips sealed, or may God strike me dead here and now as I stand in my shoes!"

Hester heaved a mighty sigh. "Cut the drivel, already; enough! Don't tempt the Evil Eye. I'll call the doctor. I'll call. But not for *your* sake, Sol. I'll do it for poor Yetta and for your grown children never to know the shame of having a senile sex maniac for a father."

Hester got busy on the telephone, and once again she made many calls to whispering anonymous sources to track down the doctor's new location. It seems he moved his abortion clinic often to keep one step ahead of the law.

At last Hester succeeded, and an appointment was scheduled for the following week. Sol kissed Hester's hands in gratitude. At this point it would seem that the story was going to have a simple, satisfactory ending, but unfortunately a quirky fate would not let it lie.

On the appointed day, Hester drove Yetta and Sol to the abortionist's clinic. As they approached the building, they saw a police van parked in front. A moment later, two police officers came out of the entrance pushing the handcuffed doctor into the patrol car.

Poor Yetta cried out, *"Oy, vey es mir,* I'm dying!" Hester quickly turned her car around and took Solomon and Yetta back to their house.

Throughout her entire pregnancy, Yetta, age forty-seven, never uttered a word of complaint or bemoaned her embarrassing condition. She simply said, "It was fated to be," and she continued to schlepp her swollen body around, cooking, cleaning, and going to the movies with Hester as if nothing in the world was going to happen.

Finally came the day when Yetta was taken to the hospital in labor. Solomon telephoned aunts, uncles, and cousins to come to the maternity ward to be with him in his time of need. The family all came and commiserated with poor Solly, while he wrung his hands and mopped his eyes. It was like a wake.

But, thanks to a merciful God, Yetta's labor was short and uncomplicated. Within two hours a nurse came out of the delivery room and announced that Yetta was just fine and the baby was a strapping, healthy, seven-pound boy.

When the infant was placed in the hospital nursery, Solomon's face suddenly took on a fatuous smile. He called the family to look in the nursery window. This feckless father, who had cursed and inveighed with fate to get rid of the unwanted baby, now pointed proudly at little Bernard lying in his crib.

"Tell me, where have you seen such a gorgeous child?" he said, in a voice choked with euphoric delight. "He's the most beautiful baby ever born, a gift from God so I should have comfort and good luck in my old age!"

As it turned out, Sol did not exaggerate. The baby was not only beautiful, but as time passed he turned out to be precociously intelligent.

In fact, he was so cute and so smart that his parents, grown brothers, sisters and cousins all spoiled him rotten. His tiny feet barely touched the ground because this worshipful family carried him around like a holy relic on a gold platter. By the time he was three years old, the results were in: "Baby Bernie" was an obstreperous, obnoxious, screaming brat whose tantrums terrorized the neighborhood.

The quiet, beautiful kinship Hester and her sister-in-law Yetta had previously enjoyed was forever altered by the noisy intrusion of a ubiquitous "noodnik," Bernard, a thoroughly no-good kid. He broke the peace, but they couldn't ignore him or evade him, so they had to learn to live with him. As Hester said, "What can we do? It's not the child's fault. My brother Solomon and his family took a perfectly good baby and made from him a goddamit."

FLEUR W. TAMON

uhm . . . take your legs for example. why, if it weren't for your legs, your genitals would be down there in the dirt.

DIANE GERMAIN

CIVIC DUTY

Dykes to Watch Out For

ALISON BECHDEL

Witness

I admit it, I don't do shit.

I never do.

I adopt a "wait and see" attitude.

Most of the time these things just go away by themselves. Why jump to unnecessary conclusions?

I sit up in bed. I buff my nails. I try to guess where those ear-piercing screams are coming from. The garden below my window? The park? The TV next door? It's fun to play detective.

A woman getting bludgeoned to death and a cat in heat sound remarkably similar.

It's easy to be fooled.

Rooftop slaying or children playing?

Most people don't realize dialing 911 costs 50 cents. Let the neighbors call.

Probably nothing more than some slut fucking.

I pick up the receiver, I put it down again.

In the park I hold the *Times* in front of my face. What is that couple doing over there? Are they struggling or *dancing*? Vicious assault or April Fool's Day gag?

It's not polite to stare.

I never take a stand until I've heard both sides of a story.

She runs away, he catches up, pins her to the ground, a knife to her throat. I glance at my watch, I've got to be going.

Nobody likes a busybody.

I pull my hat down over my face and walk toward the nearest exit. Only cowards run.

Victim of rape or eager and willing? Hey I'm not one to spoil somebody else's party.

One foot in front of the other. That's how I make tracks.

The bitch probably deserved it.

Actual cries for help or attention-seeking publicity hound?

I shout out the window, Okay, I heard you the first time! Would you shut up already? I've got to get some shut-eye or I'm going to look like shit tomorrow.

To avoid stray bullets I stay close to the floor. Reach up, slam the window shut.

What ever happened to those silent killers of yesteryear? They'd do their job swiftly and efficiently, and the rest of us still got a full night's sleep.

She sent him mixed signals. She wanted it, she didn't want it. The cockteaser.

Mugging in progress or "Trick or Treat" time?

The school bully offered me $1.00 to keep my mouth shut after I spotted him setting fire to the girls' locker room. Pal, I said, make it $1.50 and you've got yourself a deal.

"Officer, it was impossible to tell what he looked like with that stocking mask on."

"Which way did he go?" Like the scarecrow, I wrap my arms around myself and point in opposite directions.

Manslaughter or fraternity initiation rite?

They're probably just filming another episode of *The Equalizer*.

I live above a crack factory. They don't bother me, I don't bother them. I pound on the wall, they turn their stereo down. We respect each other's privacy.

Nobody likes a tattletale.

So he slaps her around a little.

I say to the guy reading the newspaper next to me, Do you see what I see? He says, Do you see what *I* see? We shudder. Teamwork.

We agree. Serves her right for taking a walk so late at night in a changing neighborhood.

He should have given him his wallet the first time he asked.

Sometimes you get what's coming to you.

A hit-and-run. I watched a black sedan speed away in a cloud of dust. Sorry officer, I said, I had the license plate memorized, couldn't find a pen, then I forgot it.

Preppie murder or was she "hurting" him?

Check out what she's wearing! The whore.

From a safe distance I size up the assailant. Isn't it the thought that counts?

I could go to a lot of trouble for nothing. What if my photograph doesn't get in the paper? The mayor doesn't praise my heroism?

Rule: I never intervene if I'm on my way to the office. I'd mess up my suit.

Six of *them* against one of *me*? I'm not crazy!

What, with my own bare hands?

He could have a gun.

I stumble upon a body. Critically wounded as a result of multiple stab wounds or homeless bum taking a nap? Tiptoe away.

They could say I did it. A case of mistaken identity. It's uncanny the way the police sketch looks exactly like me. They'll lock me up, throw away the key.

In the morning a cardboard figure lay in the grass where the girl had been murdered. The neighbors and I looked at each other with surprise, "I thought *you* called."

Don't blame us. Blame the system.

We're good people. We're a community. We donate money to the Wildlife Preservation Fund each year. We *care*.

Nothing like this has ever happened in our neck of the woods before.

What a shame. She was such a lovely girl.

Oh well, that's life in the big city.

That's par for the course.

If you can't stand the heat get out of the kitchen.

A cop at my door. He asks me questions. I cut him short. Officer, I say, I'm one of those lucky people who can sleep through anything.

LISA BLAUSHILD

N. LEIGH DUNLAP

Jury Duty

I had spent the first part of the summer distraught, writing a story about a woman I know, a lesbian, who had a baby. I wanted to do the subject justice, nothing preachy or high-toned, just honest observation and discussion. The story was boring. It was boring to me when I was writing it, and I assumed it would be boring to anyone who might read it. Brenda and Mary were portrayed as loving, concerned future parents, the problems of pregnancy discussed with sympathy. Integrity was my byword. In my story Brenda was fertilized at a medical center by a doctor she called The Inseminator. The best scene involved the couple sitting at the breakfast table, sharing a muffin, telling insemination jokes. They weren't male stand-up comic jokes that someone like Tom Driessen might tell, but a scenario involving a series of movies called *The Inseminator*. Arnold Schwarzenegger would fertilize whole cities, metropoli, continents. This was the comic relief. In art, as in life, accidents happen, and Brenda lost her baby. I kept hoping as I wrote the story that I wasn't punishing her by resolving the plot in that way. I went through the list of all my friends who'd miscarried and felt reassured that at least in real life justice plays no role.

Then two things happened. First, my good friend Lois told me that the woman on whom I'd based Brenda had fallen in love with the man who'd gotten her pregnant. In real life Brenda hadn't gone to a doctor at all. She'd gone to the Drake Hotel, and when her basal temperature was perfectly adjusted, had made love to her friend's friend, Mark, a book designer. She's the kind of person who cuts corners. Her night of heterosexual passion led to Kyle, who's now almost two, and is said to resemble Mark more strongly than Brenda. Meanwhile, Mark had begun to call. It was only natural that he'd be interested in his son. They had dinner a few times and one thing led to another. Now Brenda's wearing makeup again, seeing Mark regularly, and having very little to do with Mary, the woman with whom she was supposed to be raising Kyle.

Lois spared no details. The makeup she can accept. After all, who doesn't want to look nice? Why should women deny themselves what's best from the past to make a statement about the present that's finally puritanical? "No, the makeup is great," Lois said. "Besides, even men wear makeup these days. My butcher wears something that keeps his skin looking tight and young. It's the damned shoes."

"The shoes?" I asked.

"She buys shoes to match all her outfits now. She's a regular Imelda. And the hair. It's sleek. It's contemporary. It could co-anchor the news without a face to hold it up."

"Good for her," I said, thinking that my story was probably too weighty and moralistic. "As long as she's happy."

"Good for Kyle that the father's interested. Old Brenda's too ditzy to raise that child herself."

"So it's a happy ending."

"Not really. It's a crying shame. Why is it love that always changes women? Even in the highest art. Even in Jane Austen. Why can't it be nautical adventure, or politics or ideas?"

I was thinking this over Monday morning when I arrived for jury duty. It was the Municipal Court, where I hoped I might get involved in a short, interesting case that would yield a story. Twelve weeks on Claus Van Bulow didn't appeal to my immediate sense of my future self. I had stories to write, dinners to cook, a tennis backhand to improve. Give me a small murder, I thought, an unambiguous kidnapping. Give me a purse thief with musical abilities or a man who's pruned his neighbor's tree while high on angel dust. Let me be out of here by rush hour.

I spent nearly the entire week of jury duty sitting on the bench. Twice I was asked not to read. Many potential jurors snored blissfully around me. None were asked not to sleep. The third time I began reading nobody bothered me. I was set in my ways. Besides, the book was non-fiction. I was a serious person. The book's cover was navy blue. The title was engraved.

While sitting on the bench waiting to be called, I spent part of each day staring at a pregnant woman. She was small and dark, maybe Indian or Pakistani, and sweated profusely. I wondered if she really had to endure the week or could have used her pregnancy as an excuse. I wondered if she would have liked my story about Brenda. I began thinking of pregnancy itself as a form of jury duty. I remembered when I had my first child. The nurse held her up to my face, but because I wasn't wearing glasses and was dopey from labor, I thought the nurse's elbow was part of my daughter's back, a protrusion. "She's beautiful," they assured me, but I was overcome by fear and unable to ask about what I suspected until a second viewing.

At the time of my jury duty I was on a medication for my nerves. I'd been having panic attacks in unlikely places. One, for instance, had been in a women's locker room at a YMCA. Its origin remained a mystery. The others—before speaking to audiences, while driving to work, visiting my mother at the hospital—I could explain. Not understanding my latest one sent me straight to my physician.

"Can you help me?" was all I wanted to know.

Before he answered, he made his eyes small and meaningful and told me all about his own panic, panic while giving a medical paper on liver disease, panic at his father's funeral.

"Did he have liver disease?" I asked.

"A boating accident," he replied and wrote me a prescription for a new drug that nips panic in the bud. No more adrenaline coursing through my system like a commuter train to Tokyo. It was his metaphor, and I thanked him.

The trial on which I actually served as an alternate involved a gang shooting in February. I mention the month because crimes of passion seem barely plausible in winter. A bloodless killer, I concluded, a sociopath. Even before the gun with his fingerprints had been introduced and the witnesses gave their testimony, my mind was made up. I'd rewrite the story. Mary would kill Brenda for having betrayed her. It was plausible. It was justice. It would happen in August.

MAXINE CHERNOFF

Supreme Court Roundup

Washington, May —*The Supreme Court took the following actions today:*
FIRST AMENDMENT

In a landmark decision, the Court ruled unanimously in favor of a twelve-year-old plaintiff who sought damages on account of being denied the chance to audition for the Clint Eastwood role in the motion picture *Maddened Rustlers*. The Court's opinion, written by Chief Justice Happ, argued that exclusion of the little girl was "tactless." The case was not decided, as had been expected, on the ground of sex discrimination; rather, the Justices invoked the First Amendment's guarantee of freedom of expression. The Court thus affirmed for the first time the constitutional right to a screen test.

SEARCH AND SEIZURE

Overturning the "dog's breakfast" doctrine of search and seizure, the Court held unconstitutional the Drug Enforcement Administration's system of obtaining search warrants, under which a judge who issues a warrant receives a warm, wet kiss on the mouth, while a judge who refuses a warrant is reclassified as a Controlled Substance. Justice Happsberger, writing for the majority, said that such procedures "lean upon the delicately coiffed maiden of the Fourth Amendment with the great ugly brutish heavily muscled shoulder of procedural error," and cited Judge Cheerful Hand's famous dictum "I shall keep at it with these metaphors till I'm old and it's unbecoming."

TAXES

Without hearing arguments on the issue, the Court ordered the Internal Revenue Service to desist at once from collecting personal income taxes—a practice that Justice Hapenny defined in his opinion as "a crying shame" and "the product of diseased minds." He pointed out that the government could easily collect the same amount of money by manufacturing and selling wall plaques that say "UNCLE SAM LOVES YOUR FIRST NAME HERE."

CONTROVERSY

In one of their occasional "piggyback" decisions, the Justices resolved some of the long-standing issues that clog the Court calendar. They ruled that nurture is more influential than nature, that men make history, that Iago is driven by motiveless malignancy, that one isn't too many and a thousand is enough, that there is an earthly paradise, and that Don Bucknell's nephew Ed doesn't look anything like Richard Gere. Justice Hapworth dissented but was too polite to say so.

MORAL BLIGHT

Citing "want of attractiveness" as a reason, the Court declined, 7-2, to hear an appeal by the publisher of two so-called men's magazines, *Rude Practices* and *Men's Magazine.* In the majority opinion, Chief Justice Happ explained that appellant's arguments were "unprepossessing and—let's be frank about it—just incredibly disingenuous." Dissenting, Justices Happer and Happner said they wanted to pretend to hear the case and then "fix appellant's wagon" for "putting out such typographically unappetizing publication."

In a related decision, the Justices unanimously refused to hear a song written by a Kleagle of the Ku Klux Klan.

CRIMINAL

By a 9-0 vote, the Court held unconstitutional a New York City statute that would have mandated criminal convictions for suspects who fail to take policemen aside and "read them their duties." The statute had required that suspects deliver these "Caliban warnings" to policemen in order to remind them of their power of life and death, their obligation to attend to personal hygiene, etc. The Court, in an opinion by Justice Happell, contended, "Who can doubt that this would be the first step toward compelling suspects to serve their arresting officers creamed chicken on toast points?"

GIBBERISH

The Court voted unanimously not to review a case in which a court of appeals struck down a lower federal court's decision to vacate an even lower court's refusal to uphold a ruling that it is not unconstitutional to practice "reverse discrimination." Chief Justice Happ, who wrote the opinion, said that the Court "is not, nor will it consent to be, a body of foolosophers easily drawn into jive baloney-shooting." The Modern Language Association filed a brief of *amicus curiae* ("friendly curiosity").

GREED

Splitting 8-1, the Court upheld the constitutionality of a federal program for the redistribution of wealth. Under the program, which is known as "horizontal divestiture," rich people are asked to lie down, and poor people then divest them of their money. Justice Happold, dissenting, said that the program would diminish the impact of a standing Court order requiring that income in excess of $15,000 a year be bused across state lines to achieve bank-account balances.

As is their custom, the Justices closed the session with an informal musicale, playing a Corelli *gigg*. Justices Hapgood, Hapworth, Happner, and Happer performed on violin, Justice Happel on bassoon, Justice Happsberger on harpsichord, Justice Happold on oboe, Justice Hapenny on flute, and Chief Justice Happ on *viola d'amore*.

VERONICA GENG

MEN
(MALE-BASHING)

MARY LAWTON

Rachel Samstat's
Jewish Prince Routine

You know what a Jewish prince is, don't you?
> (*Cocks her eyebrow*)

If you don't, there's an easy way to recognize one. A simple sentence. "Where's the butter?"
> (*A long pause here, because the laugh starts slowly and builds*)

Okay. We all know where the butter is, don't we?
> (*A little smile*)

The butter is in the refrigerator.
> (*Beat*)

The butter is in the refrigerator in the little compartment in the door marked "Butter."
> (*Beat*)

But the Jewish prince doesn't mean "Where's the butter? He means "Get me the butter."
He's too clever to say "Get me" so he says "Where's."
> (*Beat*)

And if you say to him —
> (*Shouting*)

"in the refrigerator" —
> (*Resume normal voice*)

and he goes to look, an interesting thing happens, a medical phenomenon that has not been sufficiently remarked upon.
> (*Beat*)

The effect of the refrigerator light on the male cornea.
> (*Beat*)

Blindness.
> (*A long beat*)

"I don't see it anywhere."
> (*Pause*)

"Where's the butter" is only one of the ways the Jewish prince reveals himself. Sometimes he puts it a different way. He says, "Is there any butter?"
> (*Beat*)

We all know whose fault it is if there isn't, don't we.
> (*Beat*)

When he's being really ingenious, he puts it in a way that's meant to sound as if what he needs most of all from you is your incredible wisdom and judgment and creativity. He says, "How do you think butter would taste with this?"

(Beat)

He's usually referring to dry toast.

(Beat)

I've always believed that the concept of the Jewish princess was invented by a Jewish prince who couldn't get his wife to fetch him the butter.

NORA EPHRON

KATE GAWF

A Name

Suppose your parents had called you Dirk. Wouldn't that be motive enough to commit a heinous crime, just as Judys always become nurses and Brads, florists? After the act, your mom would say, "He was always a good boy. Once on my birthday he gave me one of those roses stuck in a glass ball. You know, the kind that never gets soggy"—her Exhibit A. Exhibit B: a surprised corpse, sharing a last moment of Dirk with the mortician. And Dad would say, "Dirk once won a contest by spelling the word 'pyrrhic,'" and in his alcohol dream he sees the infant Dirk, all pink and tinsel, signing his birth certificate with a knife. Still, Dirk should have known better. He could tell you that antimony is Panama's most important product. He remembered Vasco da Gama and wished him well. Once he'd made a diorama of the all-American boyhood: a little farm, cows the size of nails, cottonball sheep, a corncob silo, but when he signed it Dirk, the crops were blighted by bad faith. Too bad. And don't forget Exhibits C, D, E . . . The stolen éclair, the zoo caper, the taunting of a certain Miss W., who smelled of fried onions. It was his parents' fault. They called him Dirk.

MAXINE CHERNOFF

NICOLE HOLLANDER

Men: What Makes Them That Way?

I have finally figured out why men are the way they are. It was just one of those fortuitous things, like Franklin figuring out lightning, or Newton being struck by gravity. Only more useful.

We live in the Information Age, right? We are what we know, and media make the man. So where are men getting the information that is making them think, talk, act and look like they do?

Not from newspapers, because the men who read newspapers read the same ones read by women. The same goes for TV and movies—they're not gender-specific, and if the garbled messages were coming from them, women would act the same way men do.

Which, of course, we don't.

Only one mass medium is divided into men's and women's sections: magazines.

When my train of thought pulled into that station, I jumped off, ran to the nearest newsstand and purchased copies of *Esquire, Playboy, Gentlemen's Quarterly, Field & Stream, Soldier of Fortune* and *Man's Life*.

Talk about your dimestore revelations. Any woman who bothered to skim through my collection of man-zines would have seen it as clearly as I did. No wonder men are the way they are!

Of course, it would be unfair to say that all men are alike. Not at all. But most men do fall neatly (for a change) into one of, say, six categories. And there's a magazine for every man.

Esquire: Man at His Best

I'll humor *Esquire's* "Man at His Best" claim and put it at the top of the heap. But I'm skeptical. The magazine has a regular department (also called "Man at His Best"—Lesson No. 1: Men's mags are no place for subtlety) dedicated to helping guys out with some of the really tough parts of modern life, such as how to grill a fish or buy boxer shorts. "(Cary) Grant wore silk underpants, as *Esquire's* George Frazier revealed almost 30 years ago," pants the Rona Barret-like prose. Now, if this is the kind of information "Man at His Best" needs, the rest are in BIG trouble, yes?

Speaking of BIG, there's *Esquire's* annual fiction issue, where a lot of the stories are about The Big One, which was a war, *the* war, the *good* war, the war that will *never, ever* end in certain literary locales.

Between the silk underpants and the obsession with The Big One, I'd say all those men who seem perfectly normal at the office but turn out to have major hangups that only emerge after dark are probably *Esquire* readers.

Playboy: Entertainment for Men

Some say the only right thing to say about *Playboy* is that it demeans women. Maybe so. But when I think of "demeaning" I think of being a waitress in a truck stop where guys do things to you that Playboy centerfolds only have done to their pictures. And then they leave you a lousy tip.

We can each think what we please about *Playboy*. At least it doesn't sublimate sex with a lot of tripe about silk underpants and The Big One. And after about a zillion scholarly studies, the only thing anybody knows for sure about the effects of those centerfolds on men is that they cause erections. Which men would probably get anyway.

I didn't actually read any of the articles in *Playboy*. I figure men don't either.

GQ: For the Modern Man

This is the magazine for young men who will grow up to read *Esquire*. The junior-class textbook includes articles about Captain Kangaroo ("still rolling along") and orthodontia. (I'm not kidding —both in the same issue.) As a prerequisite to how to grill a fish, there's how to cook a catfish.

This is what I mean about magazines explaining why men are the way they are. In the past, men cooked spaghetti (dinner) and omelettes (breakfast). Now they cook fish. Ever wonder why?

GQ's speciality is filling guys in on things everybody else has known about for years, without making them feel stupid. Such as Tiffany's (No offense—I'm all for men knowing about Tiffany's), junk bonds, French Yuppies and vegetables ("they're good for you!"). So, when a young man invites you over for dinner, cooks catfish, tells you he just discovered this incredible new investment called junk bonds and asks if you've heard that there might be vitamins in vegetables . . . meet the *GQ* man.

Field & Stream

This one might be subtitled, "Man at His Best Goes Outdoors Loaded for Bear to Fight The Big One."

There's more sublimated sex, with animals replacing silk underpants. In one issue:

- "Whitetails and Scents" (about deer)
- "Trout Won't Rise? Try A Big, Bouncing Fly" (self-explanatory)
- "The Sportiest Geese of All" (Fly in from Montreal?)
- "How to Pick A Worm" (I wouldn't touch it with a 10-foot pole).

My father read *Field & Stream,* but a woman allows her father idiosyncrasies that can only be seen as idiocies in any other man.

If you find yourself sitting in a pickup truck with a guy who keeps calling you Bambi, hit the trail before deer season opens.

Soldier of Fortune: The Journal of Professional Adventurers

Last year, when everybody else had figured out that Ollie was all folly, this magazine made Lt. North a cover boy. Inside, he was surrounded by stories about Colt .45s, .38 Specials, Chinese Knife Pistols ("Deadly Duo or Toolroom Fantasy?") and M500 shotguns. Inexplicably, not a word about The Big One.

The ads feature knives, handguns, camouflage clothing, a "South Sea Island Girls Calendar" and a telephone made to look exactly like a duck. Everything a guy could need . . . on Neptune.

This magazine claims to have 175,000 readers, which is pretty scary. But if you stay out of bars with names like "The Foxhole" you probably won't meet any of them.

Man's Life: For the Modern Man of Adventure

In the Premiere Issue, the publisher promised a magazine for the man "who feels at home in a corporate boardroom as well as floating down to earth beneath the folds of a parachute."

Coming w-a-a-a-y down to earth, the lead feature was about the guy who set the world record for doing wheelies on a motorcycle.

Then there was the required article on The Big One. Plus, an article about an African safari with photos of "topless native women."

And we haven't even gotten to, "How would you like to work for the CIA? Believe it or not, the Central Intelligence Agency will accept recruits who walk in off the street."

I believe.

Advertisements offer X-Ray Vision glasses for $1.95; a Spy-Scope for $3.97; a Lottery No. Picker for $6.98; cherry bombs, whips and automatic pistols. All the things my little brother loved when he was six.

Tell the truth: Did you ever dream that those guys who share your boardroom were such adventuresome souls after hours?

A profile of a sports broadcaster began: "It's not too often in this day and age that one finds a man with his head on straight and his priorities in order."

We knew that. Now we know why.

CANDYCE MEHERANI

"WELL, YOU'RE NO JACK KENNEDY."

SHARONE EINHORN

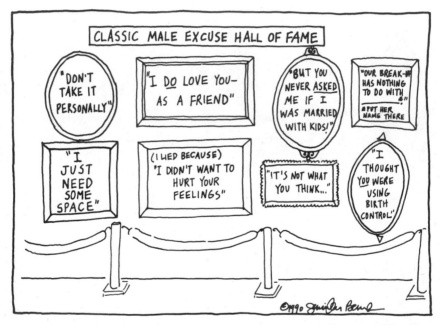

JENNIFER BERMAN

How Long Have We Two Been Together My Darling

How long have we two been together, my darling;
Connected in wedlock for life?
And through all the years you have cheated, my dear,
And you laughed at your fool of a wife.

Why this look of surprise that I see in your eyes?
Even fools can't be fooled all the time.
Though I may pretend you're my very best friend,
I have known — all this time — you are slime!

There are plenty of things that I know about you,
That you don't even know that I know;
It's so tawdry and cheap — when you think I'm asleep,
To the pub, seeking nookie, you go.

And each night you have dates, first one, then another,
With girls who make pleasing their work.
You turn some of these girls into much-too-soon mothers,
Then you leave them with child — you big jerk!

Throughout our hometown and the suburbs around
Are young bastards who look just like you,
And I face every day pitying neighbors who say,
"Poor woman . . . so dumb . . . so true-blue."

I've been biting my tongue, overlooking your sins,
Cause I thought someday you'd reconsider.
But I learned just today, one more child's on the way.
You slept with our baby-sitter!

So please understand, dear, why you see me stand here
With a knife in my hand. Duty calls!
I demand restitution, and the only solution
I can see, is to whack off your balls.

DEBRA HOFFMAN DECKER

NICOLE HOLLANDER

STONEWALL RIOTS

THE "ENVIRONMENTAL PRESIDENT"   ANDREA NATALIE

N. Leigh Dunlap

Stop And Buy the Words on a Snowy Evening

Whose words are these? "Well, I don't know."
Whose brain did off to La-La go?
Whose recollections so unclear
They make the newsmen puzzle so?

Though citizens should think it clear
There's vacant space between each ear,
No unkind comments will they make
About the leader they hold dear.

He'll staunchly vow, an oath he'll take,
"We did no wrong, made no mistake."
With actor's skill he'll make them weep,
Their gipper-god, this teflon fake.

With childish faith they go to sleep,
Entranced and duped by lies piled deep,
Fleeced once again, the nation's sheep.
Fleeced once again, the nation's sheep.

DEBRA HOFFMAN DECKER

Rose Garden Rhapsody

Read my lips: my lips I think
bear some relation to my brain.
My brain's a thousand points of light
that briefly glitter down the drain.
Read my lips! I'm as giddy
as a teenybopper in the rain.
Barbara, hold me down, and read my lips
and never let me up again,
'cause I'm just another Texas boy
from Kennebunkport, Maine.

RACHEL LODEN

DIAL-A-DYKE

The Leslie Sapphire Teen Lesbian Adventure Novel Series

The subject of sexuality is treated so unrealistically in juvenile literature that it's little wonder so many young girls wind up unhappily straight. And let's face it; most parents are straight, so any information they impart to their children is going to have that breeder bias. Because of the urgent need for adolescent fiction free of hackneyed gender roles, the Leslie Sapphire Teen Lesbian Adventure Novel Series has been created, with a socially responsible role model for the '90s.

The heroine of these unique tales is Leslie Sapphire, a rambunctious teen living in an organic separatist farm commune. She shares the homespace with her mother, a priestess in the local house of goddess worship, and her mother's lover, who is an electricienne. A haven of womanlove and nurturing, yes, but not without its share of crises. Leslie wrangles with growing pains while coming to terms with her new life—and the suburban nuclear family existence she narrowly escaped.

The series begins with *Trantrum-Prone Tomboy,* in which the pre-teen Leslie smoulders in the constraints of her typical family. After a marathon session of consciousness raising with her mother, the two make a pact to break free in *Berkeley Bound.* Mother and daughter set out for adventure and intrigue in the follow-up, *Flannel Shirts and Four-Wheel Drive.*

While settling into their new homeland, Leslie makes fast friends as she discovers a talent for organizing parties and rituals. This turn in her life is chronicled in *Training Bra Burn-In.* Leslie naturally blossoms into a sexually curious teen and her eventful coming out lasts an entire trilogy: *Gym Teacher's Pet, When Pauline Wore Patchouli,* and *Rugburn.*

An alternative lifestyle isn't all fun and games, though, and Leslie suffers her share of harassment and oppression. But to be hurt by someone of her own sex is something Leslie never expected —until it happened, in *Harlot on a Harley.*

This triggers a radical turnabout. Leslie attempts in the next book to learn just what straight life might mean. It's called *Hetero Nightmare* (parental discretion is advised).

The last book finds Leslie a little ruffled but a lot wiser. She comes to accept that harmony may be achieved in fleeting moments of prayer or sex, but that compromise and tolerance are the keys to a reasonable everyday existence. Yes, there's a happy ending, in which she moves away to attend college at Sarah Lawrence and finds true love in

THE CHOSEN FAMILY

The WONDER *if I am?* •YEARS•

starring a youthful Kenneth-Marie

I was well aware that **puberty** had me in its grip, and, with **hormones** racing, my body could betray me at any moment...

maudlin love scene

heat waves

none-the-less, I was unprepared for the curve ball that hit me squarely between the eyes when **Anya Tomas**, the new kid, walked into Miss Hunter's eighth grade class...

©Noreen Stevens 1989

the air between our desks seemed **alive** with **electricity**, making me alternately...

-stare-

tingle

+panic

she had only been in my life 24 hours and already the world seemed to be a **brighter,** more **beautiful** place with **unfathomable** potential...

wait a minute..

exactly what kind of **potential** was I thinking of ??

cont'd

NOREEN STEVENS

N. LEIGH DUNLAP

Dykes to Watch Out For

ALISON BECHDEL

Just a Phone Call Away . . .

I spent Thanksgiving on the east coast with Lori, my GLP. That's "girlfriend/lover/partner" to those of you not up on the latest of lesbian slang. (Which probably includes all of you, since I just made up the term.) We were visiting my relatives, and by the fifth day, we were suffering from an acute attack of Lesbian withdrawal.

"You know," I said to Lori, "We need support for travelers and other isolated lesbians. We need "Dial-a-Dyke.""

Think about it. All those times you've needed a quick fix of lesbian culture. Like the time you were camping at Mesa Verde, surrounded by heterosexual families, and about to kill the man two camp sites down who'd hooked up a television and a VCR. Or, that summer at your family reunion, when your aunt Madeline asked you for the sixth time, "So, when are you moving back home?"

Yup, Dial-a-Dyke is what we need, and I've even figured out the particulars. Here's how it works.

Instead of enduring a prolonged bout of irritability or succumbing to an explosive range, I merely excuse myself, dash to the nearest telephone and call the 800 number. (The cost is picked up by the National Endowment for the Humanities. Don't scoff. This is my fantasy, and I say it's a toll-free call.)

Okay, so I dial 1-800-LES-BIAN. Easy enough. Music plays, a voice sings. It's Deidre McCalla, telling us the reason why we are gathered here. I feel myself beginning to loosen up.

A new voice comes on. *Hi. You've reached the Lesbian Line, your "Homo Away from Home." I'm Robin Tyler, and for the next twenty minutes or so you are going to receive a lifesaving infusion of Lesbianism. So, sit back, relax, you're among friends.*

A pause, then new music in the background. *Bon Jour, this is Lucie Blue. I'd like to sing for you now a new song off of my album which is new also. I've trained my dog to whistle, so she'll be singing, too.* They sing for a while, then . . .

Greetings! I'm Professor Lillian Coswell, Ph.D. and it's time for Lesbian Literature. First a little trivia. Did you know that Willa Cather was a lesbian? That Virginia Woolf, and Margaret Mead had female lovers? Now, I'd like to read a poem from Audre Lorde . . .

Then Robin's back and plays a Dolly Parton and Cher duet, from the *If They Aren't, They Oughta Be* album.

After that, it's Joanne Loulan. *Hi. How are you doing? Nice haircut. Excuse me, but do you have a moment? I'd like to talk to you about your vagina. Not actually your vagina in particular, but women's vaginas in general . . .*

Next up, it's Katherine V. Forrest, who reads a sex scene from her latest detective mystery. Then Meg Christian's recording of *Leaping Lesbians* pulls me out of the fantasy I'd sunken into while listening to Ms. Forrest. By now I'm smiling widely as I hear . . .

Well, thanks for coming out! This is Kate Clinton. Think about this—which came first, the tampon or the egg?

A commanding voice follows. *Hello. This is Ginny Apuzzo, from the GLLGPCISNTF. For those of you who haven't kept up with initials, that's the Gay and Lesbian—Let's Get Political, C'mon I'm Serious—National Task Force. Here's an up-date on Lesbian news throughout the world . . .*

Well, hello. Robin here again. That just about winds up this month's Lesbian Line. Coming next month, k.d. lang and Phranc sing I Think Your Crew Cut's Swell, *then try to figure out who's the more outrageous. I, myself, will attempt to channel Eleanor Roosevelt. Oh, by the way, this isn't really an 800 number. You'll be billed 36 bucks for this call. Just Kidding!*

We're going to finish up now with a rendition of Margie Adam's We Shall Go Forth, *sung by the Denver Women's Chorus. Enjoy it, and go forth, renewed by lesbian energy.*

As the music surges, then softens, I do indeed feel refreshed. Then Robin announces: *This concludes the Lesbian Line for today. To obtain information about lesbian events in your area, press 1. To talk to a counselor, press 2. To order albums and cassettes of any of this month's performers, press 3. To increase your orgasmic response, press 4.*

I bet she's just kidding. But just in case . . .

ELLEN ORLEANS

CAREFUL, HONEY (DATING)

"Careful, honey, he's anti-choice."

SHARON NIEMCZYK

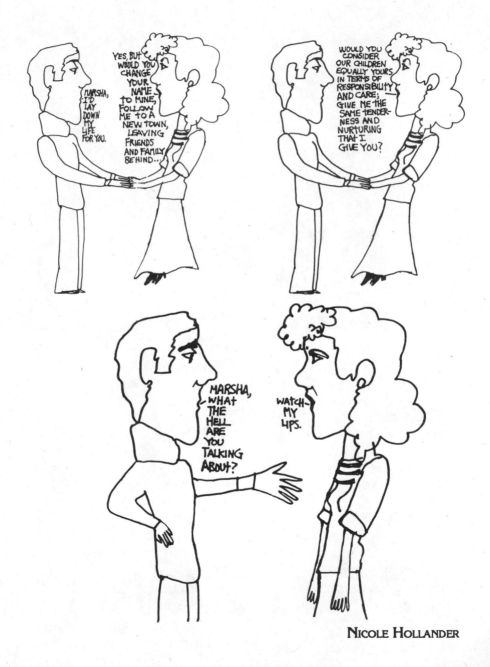

NICOLE HOLLANDER

Mail Order Love

Basically, isn't life a series of things we want, an experience for which catalogues are there to assist in the achievement of our next big purchase?

When I saw a note on the last page of *R. Team* (my favorite catalogue among the many that arrive in the mail, almost daily!) saying, "Models Available," I dialed the 800 number right away and said I wanted the blond fellow in the shorts and jersey shown painting a rowboat. He was so cute! With his hair cut short and combed straight back, his sea-grey eyes and quirky little grin, his horn-rimmed spectacles (which may have been fake, I'm not sure, since there was no distortion behind the lenses like there is with real eye glasses, but which were so appropriate as a symbol of the importance of being serious as well as playful in life), he looked studious and not at all like the kind of guy who would disrespect me for being sexually interested in him.

When I asked if he was available I couldn't believe it when the order clerk said yes. Gosh. Three days, enough time to catch a plane and taxis, and he'd be at my door. All I had to do was give my credit card number for charge at the normal rate.

I don't know what I did for the next few hours. While trying to remain cool, calm and collected—which people had so often said I was—I became hot, frenzied and dispersed until I decided it was the real me and that I shouldn't try to be cool, calm and collected any more but just wait for the model to bliss me out. When he arrived at my door he said, "Hi. I'm Jack, from *R. Team?*"

Ignoring the question in his voice, I gazed at this male I'd ordered—six feet tall, blond, well-proportioned, the grey eyes kindly above the straight nose inquisitive above the gently curving mouth hesitant. "Wow," I finally got out. "You are my dream man. You're the kind of man I'd hope to marry."

"Glad you like me." Reaching into a pocket of the light blue twill sports shorts, Jack pulled out a piece of paper and thrust it into my hand. "Here's the packing slip. Better check it to see if everything's okay."

"Let's not bother with that now." I laid the packing slip on the coffee table and took Jack by the arm. "You and I are going to have some fun."

In my car we drove to the boat harbor and watched fishermen come in with a haul. We went to the Sea View Restaurant for a lunch of broiled mahimahi and, after that, to one of our fine beaches for a romp in the waves. Jack changed from his shorts and soccer jersey into green trunks (page 6 in the *R. Team* catalogue, #62807, $23.00 plus shipping) that fit him perfectly—tight but not so tight that I didn't have plenty of room to imagine what he might look like without them. "Boy," he said, "this is the best time I've ever had on order."

A dark cloud drifted over the sunny landscape of my dreams. "You mean you've been ordered before?"

"A few times."

"But—"I frowned. "I mean—don't—"

"Why don't they want to keep me?"

"Yes." Reaching for Jack's hand, I grasped it with a pressure meant to convey that I couldn't see why any woman would want to return a model like Jack.

He sighed and picked at a grain of sand. "I don't know. There must be some reason."

"Whatever the reason, it's poppycock." Jumping up I drew Jack to the car and drove him back to my apartment. In the bedroom, I took off my skirt, my blouse. Down to my chemise, I grasped the hem of Jack's soccer jersey but he wouldn't raise his arms so I could pull it off. "What's the matter?" I asked.

"The clothes. The clothes," he said. "I always come fully dressed."

I stood back, dismayed but immediately comprehending that a model could come no other way. Sad but totally understandable. It was nothing I had to accept, either.

Marching to the coffee table, I looked at the packing slip, read the instructions for returning an order and got a pencil to fill in the blanks. There was the list of REASONS: Too tall, too short, wrong coloring, different than pictured in catalogue, changed mind since ordering, did not arrive on time, defective, didn't like styling or features, and, finally, not properly dressed. I checked 'not properly dressed.'

So Jack wouldn't see, I sealed the packing slip in an envelope. "Your style does not fit my requirements at this time," I told him. "But thanks for giving me the opportunity to consider it."

MARY S. BELL

NICOLE HOLLANDER

MARIAN HENLEY

N. Leigh Dunlap

ZANA

Bumper Stickers

"Hi! I've been waiting for you. Look at this, we've got the *same* bumper stickers! Isn't that amazing. Three out of five. We've both got *Your Karma Just Ran over My Dogma* and *You Can't Kill People by Pointing a Finger Unless You've Got a Trigger under It*. Then we both dump on Reagan. You've got *What Did the President Forget and When Did He Forget It?* and I've got *Ronald Reagan, Too Dumb to Be Guilty.* Now is that unlikely or what? I thought, 'Georgina, you've got to meet this person male or female as the case may be.' What's your name?

"*George!* I can't believe this. My name's *Georgina!* Talk about *Fate* in the Lucky Super Market parking lot!

"I see you've got *Gentle Men Let Strong Women Do It to Them.* Does that mean your preferred sexual partner is the opposite one?

"Oh boy! Well, tell me, George are you married? I don't want to be pushy, but would you like to come to dinner sometime? My God, what's going on? Look at all the cop cars!

"Right now? Well, I wasn't thinking of anything *quite* so *impetuous!*

"George, it really is not convenient for me to go with you right now. I have to get my groceries home and I have a consciousness-raising class at three.

"It is an *unwarranted assumption* on your part that I want you to come home with me *now*. But I *would* like you to come to dinner. Sometime. Are you a vegetarian?

"Oh, you are *not* a vegetarian. You *are* a bank robber. You're a bank robber?

"*You're a bank robber!*

"You've held up *two* banks and killed *eight* people . . . you *stole* this car!

"You want me for a hostage? Being a *hostage* is a very passive way to relate to . . .

"George! That's a gun! You've got a gun! Do you have *bullets* in that gun?

"Well, all right if you *insist*, but George . . . I think you should turn around.

...................?..................!!

"It's true, George. He *does* 'have the drop on you.'

"What a relief. Thank you officer.

"No, this man is not a friend of mind! We were simply discussing bumper stickers. Bumper stickers.

"Oh, George, does this mean you *like* Ronald Reagan?"

BOBBIE LOUISE HAWKINS

HOW TO KEEP YOURSELF INTERESTED

1. Keep hand gently propped under chin.

2. Keep good eye contact and raise eyebrows.

3. Keep warm, sincere smile on face.

4. Repeat the phrase, "UM-HMM" in a lilting tone.

5. Never distract yourself with your own opinions.

6. Do not yawn.

7. Do not try to understand what is being said.

8. Do not remember what has been said.

MARY LAWTON

Time Tabled

At age fifteen I used to think
The boys at school were out of sync.
The guys I then considered GREAT
Were those around age thirty-eight,
From whom of course there was no chance
I'd ever get a second glance.

So here I am at fifty-four.
Which age group do I now adore
And view as super-glamor men?
The VERY SAME ONE, chum, as then—
From whom of course there's not a chance
I'll ever get a second glance . . .

IRENE WARSAW

"Harold, I'd really prefer a wedding ring."

A.J. TOOS

Dykes to Watch Out For

Exclusive Engagement

68

© 1989 BY ALISON BECHDEL

HOW ABOUT EARLY SPRING? OR JUNE! JUNE WOULD BE ROMANTIC!

OR WE COULD WAIT FOR OUR EIGHTH ANNIVERSARY AND DO IT THEN.

WILL YOU **STOP?** WE HAVEN'T DECIDED YET WHETHER WE'RE DOING IT AT **ALL.**

WELL **I'VE** DECIDED. I DON'T KNOW WHAT **YOUR** PROBLEM IS.

CLARICE, EXCUSE ME IF I SEEM **HESITANT.** ONE MINUTE YOU'RE HAVING AN AFFAIR AND **LYING** TO ME... THE NEXT, YOU WANT US TO DRESS UP IN **WHITE SATIN** AND SWEAR EVERLASTING **MONOGAMY** IN FRONT OF EVERYONE WE **KNOW.**

WILL YOU LET GO OF THE THING WITH GINGER? IT WAS **NOTHING!** DOESN'T THE FACT I'VE BEEN IN **THERAPY** WITH **YOU** FOR SIX MONTHS COUNT FOR ANYTHING?

ALL RIGHT. I'M SORRY. BUT WHY THE SUDDEN URGE TO GET **MARRIED?** A CEREMONY WON'T MAKE US MORE COMMITTED THAN WE ALREADY ARE.

LOOK, I JUST WANNA **MARRY** YOU!

THERE. YOU GOT YOUR PUBLIC RECOGNITION. **SATISFIED?**

IT'S NOT JUST ABOUT **SECURITY,** TONI... THINK OF THE **PRESENTS!**

PRESENTS?! WELL WHY DIDN'T YOU **SAY SO?**

IT'S A **RITUAL,** TONI! IT MEANS PUBLIC RECOGNITION OF OUR RELATIONSHIP!

IT JUST HAS SO MANY **NEGATIVE CONNOTATIONS.** MARRIAGE IS ABOUT PROPERTY TRANSFER AND CREATING STATE-APPROVED **NUCLEAR FAMILIES.**

WHY MIMIC IT? WE WON'T EVEN GET A STATE-APPROVED **TAX BREAK!**

TONI, FOR US IT'LL BE ABOUT **LOVE.**

NO. FOR YOU IT'S ABOUT **FEAR.** YOU THINK A COMMITMENT CEREMONY IS SOME KIND OF TICKET TO **ETERNAL SECURITY.**

ALISON BECHDEL

PUTTING OUT THE TRASH

MARIAN HENLEY

NICOLE HOLLANDER

Putting Out the Trash

Down dooby doo down down, cumma cumma, down dooby doo down down—Hey, wait a minute! Neil Sedaka was wrong. Breaking up doesn't have to be so hard to do. That's why I've decided to share (don't you hate that word?) my helpful hints for dealing with that unwanted breakup.

First of all, change that attitude. There's no such thing as an *unwanted* breakup. If the breakup was your lover's idea, you're better off without her. If the breakup was *your* idea, go find something else to do—these tips are not for you.

Let's get started. Stop thinking of yourself as a victim. You're a survivor. After all, you survived this relationship with this horrible woman who just dumped you, and you lived to tell about it. Congratulations! Breaking up was nothing! Staying with her as long as you did was *really* stupid. You weren't her lover, you were her hostage!*

Here are a few things you can do to make that breakup a little easier to swallow.

1. *Watch cable tv.* If you don't have cable, go visit a cute friend who does. There's nothing like reruns of *The Donna Reed Show* to make you feel less stupid (unless you start watching them regularly).

2. *Quit smoking cigarettes a month or two beforehand.* Next to quitting smoking, breaking up is a piece of cake. Also, if you start smoking again, you can blame it on your brand new ex-lover.

3. *Smoke a little dope.* But not when you're crying. You won't feel any better, and it's a waste of good weed.

4. *Have casual sex.* Especially with someone for whom your hormones have raged since even before the breakup. Go ahead, you're available now. All of the fun without any of the guilt.

5. *Break your ex-lover's toothbrush in half.* But don't do this unless you're really ready to accept that the relationship's over. Also, this is most effective the first time you do it. The second time didn't do much for me, and this last breakup, I didn't even bother.

This little list will help, but, let me tell you, there's only one

---

*This is a paraphrase of one of Teresa Trull's jokes. I'm hoping that if I give her credit, even if only in a footnote, then maybe she'll invite me to lunch the next time she's in Washington. Lunch with Teresa Trull would definitely make any breakup forgettable, if not desirable.

sure-fire way to mend a broken heart. Call up a good friend, and trash that woman who's made your life hell.

Everybody wants to bad-mouth their brand new ex-lover, but few are honest enough to admit it—at least not out loud. I've always maintained that honesty is more important than honor. But you can't go around trashing her to just anyone; no, only to a chosen few. The rest of the world will continue to think you terribly mature as you profess that breaking up was a painful, but mutual, decision. They'll never suspect that *she* dumped you. They might even assume that breaking up was your idea and that you're just protecting your ex-lover's pride.

So, the secret to successful trashing lies in picking the right friend, or sister if you're lucky. Sisters are actually even better than friends when it comes to talking trash. You might think that you'll have your best friend for the rest of your life. Maybe you will, but shit happens. (I know that's a cliche, but it's true.) A sister, though, is a sister forever.

So, in between sobs, I tell my sister, "She's such an asshole."

Now, there are three probable responses to a statement like this.

First is the response you get from your mother, who just thinks you've lost a roommate. "It's not the end of the world. Maybe it's even for the best."

Second is silence, the worst possible response. This you get from misguided friends who believe that honor *is* more important than honesty. Or from a straight co-worker who's embarrassed to find you crying in the women's room. (She won't admit it, but she can't conceive that your relationship could be as meaningful as hers.) Or from mutual friends of both you and your ex-lover. Or from dialing the wrong number. Wait, let's back up here for a minute. Never, never, never trash your ex-lover in front of mutual friends. You'll look pathetic. Besides, it'll get back to your ex-lover, and she'll know that you're not handling this as well as, up until now, she's been amazed that you were. Most unbecoming. So, if you have any doubts whatsoever about the expected receptivity of your listener, call my sister instead.

So, finding the right person with whom to trash your brand new ex-lover is all-important because there's only one fitting reply to sobs of "She's such an asshole."

"She's a *fucking* asshole," my sister appropriately responds.

Now, it's important to note that your friend (or sister) doesn't have to believe that your brand new ex-lover is an asshole—as long as she can say it like she means it. Hint: After your confidante offers a particularly poignant putdown, don't push it by asking, "You really think so?!" However, the truly loyal friend will actually start believing that your ex-lover truly is the pond scum you profess her to be.

After the breakup, my therapist asks me if I've told my best friend (who also happens to be my *old* ex-lover and now lives almost two thousand miles away).

"Not yet."

My therapist is surprised. "I'd have thought you would have called her right away."

"It's only been three days," I defend myself. My therapist waits for me to go on. "Besides, she's too objective," I add. If I wanted objectivity, I'd write to Ann Landers.

"She won't trash her, huh?" This is the third breakup that my therapist has been through with me.

"Right. It's not that she doesn't want to help, it's just that she can't lie." My old ex-lover (hereinafter referred to as my best friend to avoid confusion) has never even met my new ex-lover, except over the phone. Besides, my best friend knows that my sister and I trashed her a little, too, when she was my brand new ex-lover. But that was a long time ago.

So, after therapy, I call my best friend, and she does her best. She can't bring herself to name-call, but when I tell her that now she'll never get to meet my new ex-lover, she stammers, "Well, I don't even want to meet her anymore if she's going to be like that!" Then she reminds me that I was the best thing that ever happened to her and that she was a fool to let a great catch like me get away. Christ, I've trained her well. I love this woman.

Then, my best friend's present lover, whom I've never met in person but have grown quite fond of via telephone, gets on and says, "That dumb ass. That stupid dumb ass. On my way home from work, I was just thinking what a stupid dumb ass she is."

This is pretty amazing, considering that she just this minute found out about the breakup. This woman is all right—much better at trashing than my best friend is.

So that's about it for my helpful hints for breaking up. Oh, one more thing. If your brand new ex-lover acts cold and distant when you run into her (and you're bound to eventually), just remind her that you've broken up with better people than her before. And if anybody asks—breaking up was your idea.

DEBRA RIGGIN WAUGH

SEX

"Not 'til we pass the ERA!"

SHARON NIEMCZYK & CINDY SCHUMOCK

Dr. Oops' Revised Sex Guide

By now everybody has read about Warner Books' recall of TV sexologist Dr. Ruth's *First Love: A Young People's Guide to Sexual Information.* The recall occurred when an alert librarian discovered a serious factual error that might, in fact, result in naive people becoming pregnant. Few, however, are aware of a similar but more monumental disaster that occurred when Dr. Oops was asleep at the word processor.

In what is shaping up as the most massive recall of a defective book in publishing history, Louis Chickenhawk, vice-president in charge of marketing for Ignoramus Books, announced that so far only sixty thousand copies of *Dr. Oops' Guide to Good Clean Sex* have been returned. Still unaccounted for are some forty thousand copies with the serial number 000-466. Citizens are advised to check their serial numbers and phone the special Ignoramus hotline immediately (1-800-BAD SEXX). Speaking at a news conference in Bayonne, New Jersey, last weekend, Chickenhawk promised purchasers their choice of a complete refund, a copy of the corrected guide, or a massage in Tiajuana at no additional expense.

The Guide is the handiwork of the popular, diminutive TV commentator Dr. Ona "Oops" Von Shtuppen. Speaking with her thick Franco-Prussian accent, the sexagenarian sexologist giggled, "Well, I blew it." Flanked by her husband, a muscular thirty-seven-year-old retired gardener from Long Island (referred to by *People* magazine as "Lady Von Shtuppen's laddie"), the four-foot-seven University of Vienna graduate giggled her way through the press conference, saying she was shocked that the errors in the book were not noted earlier. "I guess I was thinking of the profits and not the pregnancies," Dr. Oops allowed with her usual candor.

At first it was believed that only one factual error regarding a women's fertile time marred the otherwise insightful guide designed for young people preparing for the First Time (Please Be Kind). Subsequently, however, alert librarians across America have been putting their horn-rimmed noses to the page and uncovering numerous typos, bloops, and blunders that make the *Guide* a veritable child's garden of errors instead of eros. It is believed that many of these errors are the result of the author's attempt to simplify complex anatomical concepts and physiological processes. The book has been revised to include some of this complexity. Those who have not returned the book will certainly want to take note of the following errors.

1. On page 32, paragraph four: "The penis, a long shaftlike

structure, consists of erectile tissue enabling it to prepare for penetration." This has been corrected in the new edition to read, "The penis, an eensy-beensy to holy-Jesus-huge-sonafagun, is an Alice in Wonderland kinda organ that can go up, down, down, up, without any regard to logic or human decency."

2. On page 75, paragraph one: "The vagina is a short vaultlike structure capable of accommodating the penis for intercourse." The corrected version reads, "The vagina-bone connected to the brain-bone, the most powerful erotic instrument in the body. The right words (and they're not *open sesame*) can improve your accommodations. Otherwise it's garbage in, garbage out."

3. On page 124, paragraph two: "Oral sex is practiced by many people." This has been corrected to read, "Oral sex is practiced by many people although they don't talk about it."

4. On page 152, paragraph one: "For some females, it is necessary to say the Words, in order to arouse them." The corrected version reads, "Before attempting penetration, the male should pause and say, 'I love you. I want to marry you. You can have all my money. I will work for you for the rest of my life and do half the housework.' This is thought to be a powerful aphrodisiac."

5. Chapter Seven, "On Contraception: Don't Love 'Em If Ya Leave 'Em," begins with the sentence "Many people complain that using condoms is like making love in raincoat." This has been revised to read, "Many people complain that using condoms is like making love in a Burberry."

6. Same chapter: "Many people are excited about the new contraceptive sponge that is available and carries only a very,very minor risk of toxic shock." The revision states, "Many people are excited about the new contraceptive sponge, although some have been mistakenly using Handi Wipes instead, which is of no contraceptive value and carries a significant risk of toxic schlock."

7. Same chapter: "It is possible to make love even if the diaphragm has been left in the drawer." This has been corrected to read, "It is possible to make love even if the diaphragm has been left in the drawer, providing the male ejaculates in the drawer."

8. Same chapter: Rather than bluntly asking, "Are you on the pill? as Dr. Oops advised in the defective version, the revised *Guide* recommends that the subject be broached more tactfully. The male should stand next to the female, and without making eye-contact he should ask in an offhand manner, "So, what do you do—'ludes, uppers, downers, reds, crack, Ortho-Novum 1/50?"

9. Chapter Eight, "Sexually Transmitted Disease (STDs): Finding a Lover, Warts and All," stated, "The best way to avoid getting herpes is to insist that your partner always use a condom." This has been revised as "The best way to avoid getting herpes is to

go out and gain fifty pounds."

10. Same chapter: The old version reads, "Chlamydia, now thought to be one of the most common STDs, is often a silent infection. Women don't know they have it and pass it on." New version: "A woman should be tested for the disease and if she has it, she should greet her partner dressed as a '40s cabaret singer and begin singing, 'Tonight, my heart cries out Chlamydia . . .'"

11. The previous edition did not advise women to inspect their partners for signs of STDs. The new edition advises a complete anatomical exam. The woman should not hesitate to question any lesion she discovers. A helpful comment might be "Is that a pickle on your penis or have you got something?"

12. Men were previously told to refrain from judgment when discovering their partner had an STD. Now it is considered advisable to acknowledge the problem with a simple comment like "You filthy slut, why didn't you tell me?"

13. Page 234, paragraph three: This previously read, "Many common household objects can be used as erotic aids." To this has been appended "The blow dryer is a dangerous electronic device and has no place outside of a wash and set. Additionally, if God had wanted you to use a mango, He would have given you a mango."

14. Finally, in the most well-publicized error, Dr. Oops had advised that a woman's safest time is around ovulation, the time when an egg is discharged from the ovaries. The revised version explains that, of course, this is a very dangerous time and the woman is only safe if she can prevent the man from sitting on her egg. This proves that Mother knew best when she imparted that simple piece of sexual advice: Always keep your eggs crossed.

ALICE KAHN

Gloves

GLOVES rarely
if ever
remain
together.

Fortunately,
they do not reproduce
or what a mess
we would have
on our hands.

MARY MOLYNEUX

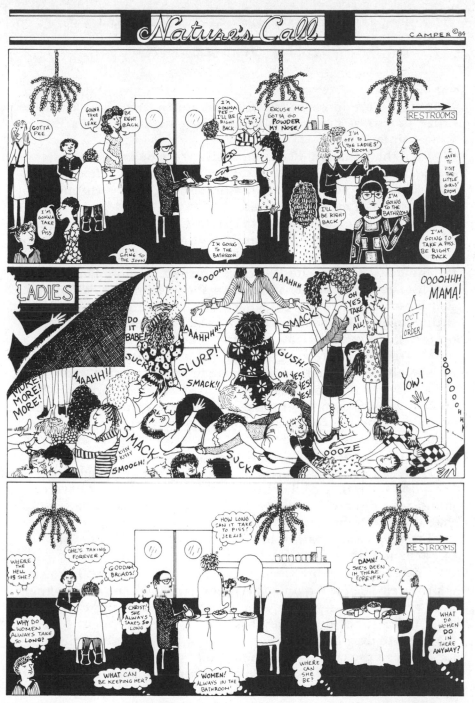

Maggie, Sex, and the Baby Jesus Too

If apologies are in order for what happened that night after the office Christmas party, then Maggie Stevens, I apologize. But, it wasn't my fault.

All right, I admit it. I've got this totally warped sense of humor. It first manifested itself when I was a child in Sunday school. That's what blew Maggie Steven's Orgasm. Honest, it was through no willful intent of my own. I swear.

As children of the pastor at First Zion African Methodist Episcopal Church, my sister Rena and I had to set an example. When Rena wanted to get back at me for something she'd often wait until the Sunday school teacher's back was turned, then imitate the way Mrs. Beasley twitched her nose when she was anxious. When Mrs. Beasley turned back around to face the class again Rena would be sitting quietly like the somber, well-behaved twelve-year-old of the pastor. I, the pastor's youngest by three years, would be trying desperately to suppress a grin. And I'd be all right too until Mrs. Beasley either twitched her nose again or asked me what was funny.

I'd try my best to straighten up by imagining somebody had kicked over the manger of the poor baby Jesus and left the infant wailing on the floor at the feet of the jackass and the three wise men. Sometimes I managed to suppress my laughter but more often I got my irreverent little butt spanked.

And I swear to you, there was no defiance involved. I know Jesus don't play that. And even if Jesus did play, the right Reverend James Scott did not. And Reverend Scott had a thick barber's strap that adequately discouraged me and my sister from ever mixing or confusing pleasure with pain. I need to make Maggie Stevens understand this.

I met Maggie at the small advertising agency where I work as copy writer. Maggie was office manager. We got to know each other well, at the small space between the counter and the copier. At least three times during my first week of employment Maggie managed to drag her hand cross my fanny when she shimmied past me between the counter and the copier.

She invited me out for a drink and we talked a bit. I discovered I liked her. She was white but she had all her racism neatly tucked in and although she didn't consider herself a feminist, she had decent politics. And she obviously had the hots for me. By heterosexual standards I was too tall, too big and too gawky. People who are unkind might even call me fat. I liked the way Maggie made me feel as if looking at me could make her pants wet. Even if I wasn't wearing a girdle.

Maggie and I flirted with each other over the heads of the heterosexuals in the office until the office Christmas party. After they opened the eighth bottle of champagne at the party, Maggie's Mums told her to ask me to dance. My Chevas Regal encouraged by my hormones told me to accept. I never win an argument with my Chevas Regal.

So Maggie plastered her pelvis to mine and made my clitoris vibrate like a rubber band. We left the party early, our arms around each other, unconcerned that we would be the juicy gossip for at least until the next office party.

It was not our fault however. It was just another torrid example of two good women once again felled by the double H: High and Horny.

Everything was fine until I noticed the chocolate colored dildo lying on the nightstand. Now I could, of course, have ignored it, but it piqued my curiosity. "Why does a white woman have a chocolate colored dildo?" I asked.

"Because I like the color," Maggie said indignantly.

I dropped the subject.

After I reached my orgasm Maggie and I were lying on black silk sheets on the queen-sized water bed in her efficiency apartment. She wore a pair of black lace panties over her blonde pubic hair. I wore only a chocolate smile.

"You think we could do something different?" Maggie asked.

"Like what?"

"Well, could you sort of hold me down and not let me up?"

"Sure, I said." And I straddled her waist and held her down by her wrist. "Is this right?" I asked.

"Yeah," she said. "I want to get up, now," she said. She also wore a leather collar and a pair of six-inch black pumps. Yes, even in bed she wore the pumps. But this was her orgasm we were working on now, I'd already gotten mine.

Maggie repeated, with a trace of impatience this time. "I said I want to get up."

"So get up, already," I said.

"No, you're doing this all wrong," she said, her pink lips pursed into a pout. "You have to say no you can't get up.

"Okay," I said, good sport that I am, "Why don't we just start all over again?"

"Great idea," Maggie said as if she'd just discovered some new strength in me that she'd overlooked before. "Now, I want to get up."

"You can't get up," I said, trying to suppress a giggle.

"Stop laughing," she said.

"I'm sorry, honey, I can't help it."

Maggie turned over on her side, with her face towards the wall.

"You're just into vanilla, aren't you?" She sounded dejected.

"Well, I like chocolate ice cream, but I think I prefer vanilla pudding and cookies," I said.

"No, I mean sexually."

"Oh, I try it all." I was not about to admit I didn't know what she was talking about.

She looked a bit disappointed. "You've never tried any, ah bondage or leather? Any water sports?" she asked.

Uh huh, I knew what water sports was. "No, I don't think I can handle water sports, but I suppose we can talk about a little bondage or leather." I pride myself on being open minded — "Just so I'm not the one that gets tied up."

Maggie reached over and grabbed the two lavender ropes tied to the head knobs of her four poster bed. She put them around her wrist and then motioned to me with her head. I straddled her again and held both her hands down. Maggie ran through her lines again: "I want to get up." she said.

"You can't get up."

"Oh, please! please! let me up!" she said. She struggled under me, but could not push me over.

"Let me up," she said again, more urgently, this time.

I let her up.

"Why did you do that?" she gave me another disgusted look.

"I thought you really wanted to get up." I said.

"No, no," she said as plaintively, as if I'd just made her miss her orgasm. "I want you to hold me down no matter what I say. I like it, Nadine," she said enunciating slowly as if she were speaking to an addled child. "I really enjoy being held down."

"I feel too guilty when I do that."

"Well, don't feel guilty. Feel guilty because you're interfering with my pleasure by not giving me what I want. Okay?"

"Okay." I was getting a little attitude myself now. Act as if you think I'm dumb and you push my buttons. I pushed her down on the bed and straddled her again. I was about ready to pee on her too if she'd asked me to.

"Let me up," she began again.

"You're not getting up," I said, as assertively as I could.

"Oh, please, please, please," she said.

"No," I said.

"Let me the fuck up," she said.

I hesitated. I don't like being cussed at. Particularly when I am making love. Apparently Maggie hadn't picked this up.

"Let me up slut," she said.

I got up off her. I wasn't sure what wired her spark plugs. But this certainly wasn't doing anything for mine. I put my jeans on and stuffed my panties into my pocket.

"Where are you going, Nadine?" She asked in that plaintive voice that meant she knew exactly where I was going and was trying to change my mind.

I leaned over and tied up my shoes without responding.

"I'm sorry, Nadine," she said. "I guess you aren't into humiliation either. My last lover was. I guess I thought . . ." her words trailed off and stopped.

"I think I'm gonna just split, Maggie," I said. "I know you tried and I tried, too, but I'm going home now."

"No, wait," she said. "Couldn't you just give me a spanking first?"

My back was to her and my hand was on the doorknob, when I heard her say, "Could you just tie me up? Give me a few lashes with a small whip or something? Bite me? I could fuck you?"

I was beginning to feel sorry for her. I really was. I turned around to say something to indicate my concerns, when I noticed her coming towards me with that chocolate colored dildo centered over that blonde patch of pubic hair, bobbing up and down in front of her. "I could fuck you?" she said, again.

I tried not to laugh; I swear I did. I mean, there in my mind was poor baby Jesus, wrapped in his blue bunting, wailing his poor little heart out on the floor of that dirty old stable again. But it didn't help.

I tried to blot out the scene of her in that black leather harness with that chocolate colored dildo bouncing up and down. But it was hard (not the dildo, although that was hard, too). What I really mean is that it was difficult not to laugh.

"You're laughing," Maggie said.

"No, I'm not," I lied.

"You are, you're laughing at me, Nadine!"

"I am not," I said with the anger of the guilty.

"Stop laughing!" She said.

"I'm sorry, Maggie." I backed down the hall, laughing and

apologizing.

Not long after that Maggie and I both found the true loves of our lives. But even now some times when I am sitting in on a meeting of the Ashley Baron Advertising Agency, and Maggie will be standing up there in her tailored black business suit trying to get the staff energized about selling high powered ads I'll imagine Maggie's pale body wearing that black harness and that chocolate colored dildo, I'll get so tickled I'll have to leave the room.

I'm sorry, Maggie Stevens. I really am.

Forgive me baby Jesus.

Perhaps I'll have to change jobs.

JULIE BLACKWOMON

Interesting Possibilities

What if food and sex traded places? What I mean is, what if we had to do it three times a day to survive, and food was something very intimate and pleasurable and you only ate with someone you really trusted, and you didn't need it to survive (though of course some would argue that fact).

So the morning fuck would be the most important one of the day. If you left the house on an empty cunt, you'd be sluggish, you wouldn't be able to concentrate, etc. etc. Lunch time—well, instead of restaurants, there'd have to be little rooms for "eating in" if you catch my drift. And for the evening meal, I guess most people would just go home. I haven't worked it all out yet, but it does have interesting possibilities.

LESLÉA NEWMAN

Self Service

There once was a woman named Doris
Who spent her time with her clitoris.
    She expertly knew
    All the right things to do,
Saying, "Anyone else would just bore us."

NINA SILVER

CHER

NICOLE HOLLANDER

Cher Gives Us A Nose Job

Why do we want to smell like Cher? That was the question in my mind as I stood crushed in with four thousand others sharing the new art form: celebrity department-store visits. Forget Godot. We were waiting for Cher.

And standing there in such close proximity to the great masses of humanity, I could not help but wonder why we would want to smell like any person.

In all the hype surrounding the unleashing of Uninhibited by Cher—in all the media stories about how Cher (despite her navel uniforms) really is inhibited, about how Cher survived those dark days when Sonny wouldn't let her wear perfume—we have overlooked the profound nature of what's going down here. Is there not some cultural meaning in the cult of celebrity odors?

I could understand wanting Cher's looks, Cher's job, Cher's agent. Cher's little boyfriend ain't bad, either. We have all heard of the "sweet smell of success," but who is to say Cher has bottled it?

There is the obvious explanation: None of us want to smell like ourselves. John Cleese, the master of embarrassing humor, exploited this fact in *A Fish Called Wanda* as he showed characters constantly sniffing their own socks, underarms, etc. We live in a world in which smelling like ourselves is a sign of failure.

As I found myself between a costume-jewelry counter and a hard place, I was amazed at what a range of people want to smell like Cher. In the crowd were businessmen in sincere suits, *grandes dames* with blue-rinsed hair, young guys in earrings, no-nonsense businesswomen in No Nonsense panty hose, Medusa-headed Cher wanabes, preppie boys, mothers with babes in arms, the rainbow coalition of multiethnic America, all shouting "We want Cher!" Could it simply be that stupidity knows no boundary?

The two security guys keeping the aisle clear next to where I stood fended off an encyclopedia of lame excuses as people tried to get up front, within smelling range of Her Cherness. "I'm with the press . . . I'm with Cher's entourage . . . I just want to go shopping . . . I MUST get through . . ." Only the lady who threw up and three others who threatened to faint were allowed through the security line.

Cher, by now twenty minutes late, was nowhere to be sniffed. But the announcer reminded us we could watch her videos on the numerous monitors set up around the store "for your convenience and for a live simulcast when Cher appears." The crowd began to boo menacingly.

Just then a stylish woman came by with a spray bottle of Uninhibited by Cher and zapped me on the wrist. Was this a new form of crowd control? One squeeze puts your mind at ease.

I thrust my wrist at the security guard, feeling that forty-five minutes of sharing our Cher space had bonded us for life. "Does that smell like Cher?" I asked him. "Smells like vanilla," he said.

A fellow sharer of our little corner of the display case, a handsome man wearing a T-shirt with a quote from Balzac, took the liberty of sniffing my wrist. "It smells more like Sonny," he said.

Suddenly the cameras began flashing like strobe lights. Cher was in the room. From where I stood, you couldn't smell her, you couldn't see her, but she walked with us and she talked with us.

For twenty minutes Cher dialogued the crowd—a half-obscene, semiliterate tease and comedy act that told me one thing. Cher is an idol because she is the kind of take-no-prisoners lady who would never spend an hour in a dangerously crowded department store to get a whiff of Cher. As she so said so profoundly when she walked out and saw the mob, "In the best of all possible worlds, this really sucks."

If there's a sucker born willing to pay to smell like Cher—it ain't her, babe. But those who lead quiet lives reeking of desperation will go to great lengths for some link to greatness. Even one that vaporizes and costs $175 an ounce.

ALICE KAHN

THE CHOSEN FAMILY

NOREEN STEVENS

"Mirror, mirror, on the wall, who's the fairest of them all, taking her age into consideration."

A.J. Toos

The Follow-Up

ROZ CHAST

Once Upon A Time

Once upon a time on another planet which had achieved an advanced state of technology, lived a beautiful young girl named Cylinderella. Cylinderella's mother had died after working for long hours in a factory under horrible conditions when Cyn was a young girl, and her father, a nuclear physicist, had remarried a horrible woman named Rosey the Riveter. Rosey had three awful daughters, who became Cylinderella's three ugly step-cylinders. The whole unhappy family lived together in pre-fab housing.

Cylinderella's new mom & three ugly steps treated the beautiful sensitive young worker like shit. They made her vacuum the entire apartment while they sat around with their feet up watching television. After coming home exhausted every night from work, Cylinderella was forced to spend hours at the Cuisinart preparing food for her new family. After dinner, it was always Cylinderella who had to carry the plates and cutlery to the sink, scrape them off, and load them into the dishwasher.

Her father, although he loved his daughter dearly, was oblivious to this unfair treatment because his mind was always preoccupied with the fashioning of nuclear technology. One wrong move and he could blow his planet to bits.

One day, a handsome young prince from planet earth landed on Cylinderella's planet. It was decided to give a lavish celebratory ball and tour of the most interesting factories and power plants for the good-looking young astronaut. Cylinderella's three ugly step cylinders and her horrid mom-substitute spent the week before the ball in a frenzy of anticipation, ordering garments from the Sears Catalog. Of course, Cylinderella was told that she had to stay home to answer the doorbell in case it rang.

However, as soon as her family had left for the ball, Cylinderella's magic fairy godmother appeared. She told the wondering young girl that her dad, the physicist, in his rush to get out of work early in order to escort his family to the ball, had left the heat on under an isotope and the entire planet was about to blow sky high. Cylinderella's fairy godmother instructed Cylinderella to hastily don a beautiful ball gown which she produced magically from thin air. Cylinderella put on the dress and rushed to the astronaut's space ship, which had been left unattended, and the two of them blasted off.

Moments later, Cylinderella's planet blew up and everybody on it was entirely destroyed.

Cylinderella and her fairy godmother flew safely back to planet earth, where the godmother was finally able to come out of the closet and Cylinderella, unemployable, went on welfare and lived happily ever after.

ARIEL TRAMWAY

✫ SLEEPING BEAUTY ✫

MARIAN HENLEY

Mother Goose Nursery Rhymes and What On Earth They Mean

The rhyme about Georgie Porgie is not too hard to understand. "Georgie Porgie, pudding and pie/Kissed the girls and made them cry./When the boys came out to play,/Georgie Porgie ran away."

Georgie Porgie is a loathsome character. He's a bully. He makes the girls cry, but then, when the boys come out, he cravenly runs away for fear they'll hit him.

Why did the girls cry? Because Georgie Porgie *forced* his kisses on them and it was intolerable to be kissed by him. He wasn't bad-looking, but he was such a *worm*.

When the boys, who had been studying (something the undisciplined and stupid Georgie never did), came out to play, they were stunned to see all the girls in tears, but when they saw Georgie Porgie running away—which he always did whenever the boys appeared—then they knew the girls were crying because Georgie Porgie had been forcing his vile kisses upon them once again.

As usual, the boys did nothing about it. You know this has happened before and will happen again. Over and over again. It's a nightmare for the girls.

Moving on to Tom, Tom, the baker's man, we find a rhyme that is a hard nut to crack. "Tom, Tom, the baker's man,/Stole a pig and away he ran;/The pig was eat,/And Tom was beat,/And Tom ran crying down the street."

It breaks my heart to limn the lines. Why should Tom of all people, be beat, and made to cry, while Georgie Porgie, a real monster, gets away scot-free?

What did Tom do? He stole a pig. As who wouldn't who worked all day in a bakery? Even delicious aromas can revolt one in time. The day comes that one longs for roast pig, and by then only an entire porker can do the job—satisfy Tom's craving for meat and his serious need for protein and electrolyte balance.

The pig was eat, the rhyme goes on to say. By whom? I'm afraid Tom didn't get any. The pig was eat—it could have been by anyone—whereas Tom was beat: we know it was Tom and no other who was beat. And Tom was strong. Have you ever tried to run with a pig in your arms? Have you ever even *seen* a mature pig? I believe the entire town turned out to beat him. It's not fair. Afterward, did he lose his job with the baker? I think so. I think that's why he went crying down the street. No amount of beating could make my Tom cry. He's crying because he lost his job and because the pig was eat before he could get any.

On to Doctor Foster.

"Doctor Foster went to Gloucester/In a shower of rain;/He stepped in a puddle,/Right up to his middle,/And never went there again."

Doctor Foster (a doctor of hydrography, by the way) is a fool. He's a fool to step into a puddle that anyone could see was a yard deep and then because of that one idiotic accident never go to Gloucester again. Did he think that if he went to Gloucester again he would step into a puddle up to his middle and that this was inevitable every time he went there? That would be particularly surprising in a doctor of hydrography. And yet isn't it true? We go to a place, something bad happens, and we never want to go back. Why go back when there are new places to go, where nothing bad has happened, like the Yucatán, which I mention only because that's where I want to go next.

I wish I could find a rhyme with a man we could all admire. Tom, Tom, even though he's a total sweetheart, is not necessarily admirable (thief and crybaby), and I know you join me in my loathing for Georgie Porgie (craven bully) and my scorn for Doctor Foster (idiot). One would think that nursery rhymes would want to set an example for infants (that's the kind of man I want to be when I grow up; or that's the kind of man I want to marry), but they don't at all, which is what's so wonderful about them. They know how men really are.

Even in "Jack be nimble;/Jack be quick;/Jack, jump over the candlestick," it is clear that Jack is clumsy and awkward, a stumblebum, in effect.

The candlestick (not many people know this) is not lit. It is not even standing upright in a holder. It is lying on its side on the floor. If Jack could jump over the candlestick (so pathetic, really), then the idea is that he might go on to jump over a box of soap and thence to the high hurdles at the Olympic Games.

Fat chance. Jack will never make it to the Olympics. No Nehemiah, he. Jack will be a Wepner (the Bayonne Bleeder), and the reason I know this is that I've just looked up stumblebum and it means a second-rate prizefighter.

The more I think about Tom, I think he stole the pig because his lover asked him to, and it was she who ate the pig. Tom wasn't beat up by the town people; he was tired. "Tom was beat" means Tom was tired. The whole adventure of stealing the pig and running away with it had wearied him, as who wouldn't it, especially after a long hard day being a baker's man. No! Now it's coming clear. He didn't work at the bakery at all! He was the *baker's man*. Her lover. He stole the pig and away he ran. To give it to the baker, for whom he'd do anything. Then he was so tired (beat) that he ran crying down the street because he felt bad about not being able to make love to the baker, who, even though surfeited with pig, wanted him to give her a cosmic orgasm.

Wait a minute! I now see that Tom, Tom didn't cry tears down the street. His was a cry of exaltation. He was whooping it up because his whole day had been such a success. He stole the pig, got away cleanly and safely with it, gave it to the baker, they *both* ate it, then they made love. Then, understandably, he was tired (beat), but he still felt great, and damned proud of himself, so he ran crying victoriously down the street, wanting the whole town to see what a man he was. He can be forgiven his vainglory. It is much better than being a fool, a crybaby, or a stumblebum.

A thief he remains. There's no way I can get around the fact, try as I may, that he stole the pig. I deplore crookedness of any kind, which is why (well, partly why) I left Dominic Racatelli.

Too bad. I love Tom. I want to portray him in the best light I can. He's a fast runner (unlike Jack), a great lover (unlike Doctor Foster). He's sensitive and caring and will do anything to please his loved one, even steal for her.

I would want to marry a man like that when I grew up. But if I were the baker, Tom, Tom's lover, I would not ask him to steal for me; I would ask him to kill for me. I would ask him to kill Georgie Porgie.

SUSAN TROTT

The Return of the Fairy Godmother.

Kate
Gawf

Suddenly, the Prince vanished into thin air, and in his place stood a brand new washer & dryer.

KATE GAWF

Turbotome

Congratulations on purchasing TURBOTOME—a software program designed especially for the Professional Writer (YOU)! TURBOTOME enables you to bypass the rough draft, the first and second drafts, the galleys—even the test of time!—and get on with the business of writing.

Let's begin with a few basic operations to acquaint you with the TURBOMOUSE.

TYPE IN a couple of sentences. GIVE VENT TO YOUR IMAGINATION!! (It's allowed.)

Take care of the pence. The pounds will take care of themselves.

Let's rewrite, using the MOUSE.

Take care of the pence and the pounds will take care of themselves.

It flows now, doesn't it? As a writer, you no doubt like to spend your time playing around with the English language. With TURBOTOME, you won't be able to keep your mouse off it!
ONCE AGAIN!!

Take care of the pence!! The pounds will take care of themselves!!

Since you've mastered the basics so quickly, it's time to get down on paper that novel you've had in brain storage all these years.
Daunted?

And how!

Don't be! TURBOTOME will guide you step by step through the arduous process. All *you* have to do right now is think long and hard about the kind of novel you might want to put your name on. (If you need more than one hour to make up your mind, DIM THE SCREEN.)

Let me write a masterpiece!

MASTERPIECE MENU

Unreadable Work of Questionable Genius
Minor Oeuvre
Commendable Contribution to the Body of Literature
Neglected Work of Genius
Classic
Nobel Prize Winner (not available with this program)

Let my masterpiece be a classic!

Good choice! And what are you going to call your classic?

"Untitled."

Immortal! It all starts with one little OPENING SENTENCE. (You may begin INPUT of your novel.)

Take care of the pence.

LEAVE A SPACE. Then TYPE IN your LAST SENTENCE. Don't worry about it being memorable. The important thing is to be able to visualize an end to the arduous process of writing your classic.

The pounds will take care of themselves.

In the space between your first and last sentences, you may BEGIN JOTTING YOUR NOTES. These should include the germ of your novel, your theme(s), and anything you want to remember to say or do during the course of it.

NOTES ON "UNTITLED"

Man's Inhumanity to Man

Man's Inhumanity to Me (would like to concentrate on my experiences in seventh grade)

Don't forget!! Dentist appointment Mon. 9:50!!

You're going to turn your attention now to the music of your prose. How would you like to be famous for your STYLE?

You bet! Let me be compared to Dostoyevski and James!

It's time to take advantage of TURBOTOME's exclusive STYLE ENHANCER.

YOUR PERSONALIZED STYLE MATRIX

despair, such   ,   ,

,whatever it was, it was certainly not finer happiness. Woe, , woe, a thrashing woe; death ... And, yet, certain things — things; these agonizingly plain. Suffering, in particular. Everything else was filthy delusion!

Isn't fiction writing exciting? Just be sure you don't leave the all-important dimension of SETTING until the last minute. Have you thought about WHERE your classic is going to take place?

India.

Great! Here are some sample paragraphs for you to embroider as you see fit:

Colonel Hatchforth, on the eve of departing with his regiment, reflected with pride on the fact that his wife was one of the few Englishwomen on the subcontinent who had never been the subject of a criminal attack or dysentery.

"We all have rituals, Mrs. Hatchforth. You English have afternoon tea and we have the Rites of Kali," Prince Begur said.

"It's not just a cow to us, Mrs. Hatchforth. It is a sacred cow,"

Prince Begur explained.

And the monsoons! The only time Mrs. Hatchforth had experienced anything like them was when she was four and her nanny left her in the tub too long.

"Why, thank you, Prince Begur, I've always possessed a longing to read the Kamasutra," said Mrs. Hatchforth.

Would you like to try your hand?

"Mrs. Hatchforth! Mrs. Hatchforth!"

Bravo! At this point, many writers like to consider GENRE. Which one are you going to choose?

The Western.

What about your CHARACTERS? How are PRINCE BEGUR and MRS. HATCHFORTH going to develop?

Through male bonding.

You're probably dying to assemble your classic! If you're anything like most Professional Writers, you find moving your paragraphs around a deeply affecting, spiritual TURBOEXPERIENCE!

But don't neglect PLOT! PLOT is the special ingredient that will give your classic LIFE!

Oh, let me think about PLOT sometime after the third printing . . .

When you're ready for a look at your WORK-IN-PROGRESS, CLICK THE MOUSE ONCE.

CLASSICS OF MODERN LITERATURE

UNTITLED

Chapter 1

"What kind of a God would allow the English to take afternoon tea?" Price Begur asked.

"I haven't the faintest idea," replied Mrs. Hatchforth, "but don't forget to take care of the pence."

Chapter XX

"There's only one man fit fer the job o' movin' a heard o' sacred cows through the Himalayas, that that's Prince Begur," Prince Begur said.

Chapter XXIV

"Won't anything make a man of you?" Prince Begur demanded of Mrs. Hatchforth after they had been on the trail a spell.

Chapter XXXII

It all had something to do with seventh grade, but neither Prince Begur nor Mrs. Hatchforth was sure what.

Page 597

"Mrs. Hatchforth! Don't forget your teeth-cleaning —"

Somewhere After the Second Climax:

"Oh, Mrs. Hatchforth — 9:50!

Epilogue

The pounds did not take care of themselves.

One of the best things about TURBOTOME is the way it simplifies the writing process so you can amass a sizable OEUVRE. And you're sure to have noticed the ADDITIONAL TIME you have during your day to create interesting material for your biographers. Why not begin INPUT of your memoirs? Right now!

For some reason I have been quite tired recently.

You're going to PAUSE now and think about the way you want to be perceived by future generations.

When you're ready to activate TURBOBIOGRAPHY, simply TYPE IN the kind of writer's life you would like to lead. Then it's back to work for you — time to put the finishing touches on your TURBOCLASSIC!

Let me put as much into my life as into my art!

Let me lead a life like Yukio Mishima's and Norman Mailer's!

YOUR PERSONALIZED TURBOMEMOIR

After scandalously ending my seventh marriage, I formed my own army yesterday, based on the belief that the old warrior ways were better. There is some dissent among the ranks as to whether this means the hoplites or the Visigoths. Anyway, I stayed up all night practicing army maneuvers in women's clothing. This was perhaps too easy a test of my manhood, as I am already a woman.

Exhausted this morning, I had to rely on a combination of Bushido and ten cups of coffee to get me through the arduous process of writing.

POLLY FROST

The Poet

She tears apart her aching heart
And shows her soul to view.
Of tragic years, in blood and tears
She writes, as she must do.
She tells of hope unrealized,
Of sorrow hard to bear,
And sells it to a magazine
To buy some underwear.

CHARLOTTE AVRUTIS KELLAR

REVISED TEXTS

Madame Bovary,
Tennis Ace

Madame Bovary's mischief-
creating boredom becomes
a thing of the past when
she discovers tennis

The Great and
Physically Fit Gatsby

The mystery man of West
Egg changes his life by
taking up running

Hamlet,
Swimmer of Denmark

The melancholy Prince learns
that he can rid himself of
anxiety and tension by
swimming a mile a day

DRAWING BY R. CHAST

The Concert

The concert hall was crowded. It buzzed unpleasantly with stiffness and July heat. I was filled with discomfort. My husband moved toward the carpeted stairs that descended to the front of the hall. He had to sit in the most crowded section of the hall between the stuffiest bald-headed man and the puffiest hair-sprayed woman so that he could see the performer's hands. My husband asked me if I was happy. I mumbled a "yes" and unwrinkled my curled program. I was wearing jeans. My husband had told me that not many people would be at the concert because of the oppressive summer heat. The woman beside me was wearing an uncomfortable looking evening dress and heels. I consoled myself that at least I was wearing comfortable clothes. I think that the woman envied my comfort, because she kept staring at me with squinted eyes and was constantly employed in moving stray pieces of her dress away from my leg.

The performer was a pianist and she was going to play a program of Franz Liszt. My husband knew every piece of Liszt's music. He was there to see if she played what Liszt wrote or if she took the simplified ossias. He never took the simplified ossias. After this performance, the pianist was going to Europe for a short concert tour. I squirmed in my hard seat. My bottom was sticking to the wood. I could feel the sweat slide down the backs of my knees. The hour for the concert to start had passed fifteen minutes ago. I felt the woman look sharply at me as I squirmed and then look knowingly at another woman on the other side of a man who looked sad enough to be her husband. I guessed that she had never experienced discomfort or heat. She looked too well disciplined in the art of boredom. I could imagine her high sharp voice as she snottily told her husband "Not tonight." He definitely did not look like he got it much. The lights blinked to signal that the concert was ready to begin.

But still we waited. I sat cramped and polite ready to applaud at the first glimpse of a pianist around the corner of the concert wall. The hush of the audience did not last. Murmurs crescendoed into the familiar hot buzz. Maybe there was not even a pianist, or maybe she had already left for Europe. The lights blinked again. The buzz diminished. I wondered if this was a ruse to make us applaud extra loudly when the pianist finally did arrive. Even if it wasn't a ruse, I wasn't going to clap. I held onto my husband's sleeve so that he wouldn't clap either. He never recognized a ruse. He would probably clap loudest. But the pianist did appear. And the applause was louder than usual. There she was in her billowy shirt and slacks. I could not help but look smugly at the stiffly dressed woman. She was in heels for nothing.

The pianist introduced the pieces that she was going to play; then she explained the pieces she was going to play. I could already feel my attention wandering. The program had not said that the concert was annotated. I would now be lucky if I got home in time for Johnny Carson. The pianist began to play. I listened carefully to the first few lines. My husband had performed this piece. It was *Sonetto del Petrarca*. She was playing it all wrong for my ears. It was definitely going to be a long night. My husband shifted in his seat uncomfortably, leaned toward my hair that was plastered against my ear, and whispered that she just took an ossia. I wondered how many other people in the audience realized that she was not playing what Liszt actually wrote. I turned in my seat and searched the faces around me. They were all staring hard concentrating on the pianist with pleasure on their faces. I could not believe that all of these people thought the concert enjoyable. And I was right. A little girl below me in the front row was staring wistfully at the red 'exit' sign. I watched as she whispered to her mother and as her mother whispered angrily back shoving an unwanted coloring book into her hands. The child let the book fall to the floor and then settled to take a nap against her mother's side. She, also, knew that it was going to be a long night.

People clapped around me. I looked on the program. She had three more pieces then intermission. Maybe we could leave at intermission. I thought about the baby squirrel I had seen that day outside the study window. I had never seen a baby squirrel before and had often wondered where they went between birth and adulthood. I had never seen a book explaining the lives of squirrels. They seemed always to get only half a page and a picture in a book of New England animals. I hadn't even heard of people studying the lives of squirrels like I had about people studying gorillas, chimps, lions, and elephants. Maybe New England animals just weren't as exciting to live with as African animals. Although, I had recently seen a book in the book store of a woman who had lived with a family of beavers for four years. Maybe someone could become a part of a squirrel colony and be accepted in their rituals. I had always wanted to be accepted into a group that no one else had ever been accepted into before. I really admired Dian Fossey and Jane Goodall. Maybe if I sat for a few days by the tree where I had seen the baby squirrel, I would become accepted and the squirrel would let me in on his secrets. I imagined myself climbing the tree and building my own nest. It would be cool in the trees. I had never seen a squirrel keeping still because of the heat. They were always bouncing among the branches. Maybe the squirrels would begin to sit with me or show me where they hid the bread and pizza crusts that I so often put out for them. My husband nudged me, "She just left out a page of the *B minor Sonata.*"

My mind returned to the concert hall. I felt as if my mind were like one of those old-fashioned dolls where the face turns inside the head and clicks into place for a new expression. This esteemed pianist had left out a page of music and I had missed it because I was imagining myself as part of a squirrel colony. I looked around to see if anyone else had noticed, but they were all staring ahead with smiles of excitement and admiration on their stiff, fake faces. I could not believe that they were not pretending this interest. It was unnatural in this heat. Although, probably, these were the same type of people who never looked up during a prayer to see if someone's eyes weren't shut. Maybe *I* was unnatural for being affected by my hot, sticky, stuffy, oppressively unbearable wet environment. Maybe I was wrong to feel that all activities should be cancelled that didn't include water and air conditioning in the summer. Maybe I shouldn't be getting really angry at my husband for bringing me here to sit for two hours to feel the sweat run down my legs and between my breasts.

I concentrated my focus directly on the pianist. She was bent awkwardly over the keys as if the bench were too far away from the piano. As I stared, it seemed that the bench was getting further away from the piano and that her face was getting closer to the keys. I imagined everyone's surprise if the bench slid entirely away; if someone took the bench away, it would be funnier. Or, what if someone pushed her face into the keys as it was so close already. I imagined the crashing, dissonant notes as her face hit. My husband nudged me, "This is embarrassing."

I whispered grumpily back, "Does that mean we can leave at intermission?"

"No, I want to see what she does to the *Dante Sonata.*"

But people were clapping and whistling in great excitement. The "bravos" were yelled from all directions as she finished with a colorless chord. She curtsied and disappeared. She reappeared with more curtsies, more bravos. I felt sick from the increased movement around me. The hot air was thick with hair spray, perfume, and bug lotion.

My husband leaned again toward my sweaty side, "These people are musical idiots." But he was clapping also.

Finally she stayed hidden and the clapping stopped. The lights came up and the people stood with exclamations of the highest praise. I listened for a while to a young man and woman behind us who were discussing the pianist's ability to be able to play so much from memory. "Her memory is incredible," the young blond woman remarked. "I have been playing for six years and I still have a hard time memorizing the circle of fifths." From the sound of her voice and the place her hand was resting, I guessed that it could not be the piano that she had been "playing" for six years. But there was no time to listen longer, because the lights blinked, and, by this time, I recognized the blinking lights as a warning for what was to come. The people slithered back into their places and the sounds of their uncomfortable clothes hissed as they scraped against the seats. I tried to ease my wet, cramped legs and concentrated on the piano. The line "I settled down for a long winter's nap" drifted through my mind. I wished it were winter. I had four more pieces to sit through. I asked my husband how much longer the concert would last, and he said that if she didn't leave out any pages, it would last forty-five minutes. The lights blinked their last warning.

There she was just the same in her billowy shirt and slacks. More curtsies, more introducing, more explaining. My eyes focused on the two outlets in the hardwood floor in front of the piano. The outlets began to merge into one another and form one large indefinite floor outlet. But, as the outlet shimmered before my unblinking eyes, it looked like one large indefinite eye. A giant cyclops looking at all of us out of his one big watery eye. Wondering why we were all sitting on his face. But, not only why we were all sitting on his face, but why there was a woman in a billowy shirt and slacks making such a nuisance of herself on his forehead? And in this heat? I sympathized with the cyclops and thought that Odysseus may have acted too quickly when he struck an unconscious cyclops in the eye with a post. The music stopped and the clapping began again. Why did these people have to applaud between every piece? It made each piece longer by at least five minutes on each end. The forty-five minutes that my husband had quoted me did not include applause.

The *Dante Sonata* was the last piece on the program, but it was long. At this point I didn't care how long it was; I was just glad that she was finally playing it. My husband wasn't really listening any-more either. He was studying the little girl in front of us who had long since given up the idea of a nap and was, instead, making faces at her mother and kicking her seat. I vowed never to make my unborn children sit through a concert that they did not want to go to. In fact, I would stay home with them. The next time my husband wanted to see if someone took the ossias, he could go see himself. My husband must have sensed my decision, because he whispered that he was glad that I had gone with him and that he was glad it was almost over. And it was. The bravos began and the whistling and the clapping and the stamping and then the curtsies and the disappearing and the reappearing. I found my crumpled program, and clapped with relief. I still had an hour until Johnny.

HELEN PEPPE

Piano Lessons

When I was eight, Aunt Margaret bought Ellen a whole piano in honor of her twelfth birthday and also because Aunt Margaret wanted their lives to be surrounded by the sounds of beautiful music. She said she wanted to give me the same great opportunities Ellen had and that if Mom would just pay for my lessons, I was welcome to practice on their piano. Aunt Margaret told Mom I had begged her and begged her to please let me take the lessons with Ellen and she couldn't bear to see me be underprivileged, but I don't remember ever begging her to let me take any piano lessons. And even if I did, I was only in third grade. Later Mom found out that the actual reason Aunt Margaret wanted me to take piano was so she could get a cut rate for bringing the teacher another kid.

The teacher was this lady whose apartment smelled like a lot of cats. She lived downtown on a street with bums walking on it, and when we would pass one my Aunt Margaret would look at the bum and then look at me and Ellen to make sure we could see how much she was willing to suffer in order for us to learn the piano.

Aunt Margaret would stay until after Ellen's turn, and then they would leave to go wait for me at the Woolworth's lunch counter, and I would be alone with the music lady who naturally scared me because she was always talking loud and sweating big sweats under her arms and yelling "Tempo! TEMPO! goddamn you!" She would grab my hand and pound out the time with it like I was too stupid to count. It was always the same song over and over. *Ten Little Indians*. Ellen was already on *Carnival in Venice*, and I was still stuck playing *Ten Little Indians*.

After my lesson I would walk down First Street three blocks fast, following my aunt's instructions to quit my bad habit of stopping to stare at interesting people. Then I'd turn up Cresswell Avenue, go one block, then go into the Woolworth's, walk through the candy, the makeup, the ladies' nightgowns, then over to the counter where Ellen would slide off her stool and tell me what she just ate.

I was supposed to practice more than I did, but Uncle Jim developed a problem of not being able to stand the sound of the piano when I played it. And then before I knew it, it would be the day to walk past the bums again.

Lucky thing for me something happened to that lady. Who knows what, but we went there one time and knocked and knocked and finally a man in an undershirt opened the door behind us and said, "She moved. Do you mind?"

LYNDA BARRY

Empress

You wake up in the morning, have a cup of coffee, and begin to feel pretty good about life. You're young (relatively), you're healthy—just like your mother always says. Maybe you even have a great job and a man in your life who, while he doesn't have a job, is absolutely certain he's heterosexual. You say to yourself, "It doesn't get much better than this."

You open the newspaper: The upper atmosphere has been eaten away by hairspray; therefore, the average daily temperature in August will be 127 degrees. A savvy tour company is offering "Husband Hunting Safaris" to Third World countries. The cereal you ate every morning as a child has been found to cause slow-but-steady brain damage starting at age 30. Harvest gold and avocado green are the hot new colors. Sylvester Stallone is making another movie.

You shake off the news. After all, the newspapers are always full of tragedy. Life goes on.

The phone rings. It's the IRS. It's about that $31.50 you made babysitting for Mrs. Paisley back in 1977. With interest and penalties, you owe $3,869.99. If you don't have the cash, they'll take your car.

You go outside to get in your car to drive to your great job. You notice that your car no longer has a stereo. Also, there's a large hole in the driver's side window, and a lot of broken glass. You make a mental note to call the IRS and let them know where to find the car.

Not yet convinced it's all hopeless, you get on the bus, sit on something sticky and wonder if you'll be attacked by the young man wearing camouflage fatigues, cradling a Howitzer and drooling heavily.

You arrive safely at the office—things are looking up. Until your boss tells you the company has been bought out by Sleaze-o Ventures. There'll be no more cost of living raises, and the receptionist was let go, so you'll have to handle the phones for a while. But only for six months, after which your entire division will be liquidated. Madeleine, the airhead who sits next to you, has brought in her wedding album.

Somehow, you make it through the day. You take a taxi home and collapse to read your mail. There are no letters from friends. Your credit card has been charged three times for a sweater you only bought once.

Figuring you have nothing left to lose, you check your answering machine. The landlord can't find a plumber to fix your toilet before next Friday. Your man saw that Zefferelli movie about St. Francis on late-night TV and has decided to become a Franciscan monk.

You seriously consider the possibility that aliens abducted you while you slept, and have imprisoned you on Planet Unbearable. You are seething with free-floating rage and frustration. You want to kill. You want to cry. You want to take over the world, and *make things work*. You want people to behave as if they have human-sized brains and just a tiny bit of class.

Well, when *I* have A BAD DAY, there's a game I like to play called "When I Become Empress of Everything." It's a game about getting in touch with your lust for power and straightening out everything that's wrong with the world. It's a game for only one player, which is handy when everybody else is acting like a jerk. I bet you would enjoy it, too.

All you do is, get out a legal pad and at the top of the first sheet write: *When I Become Empress of Everything*. Then, start writing down what you'll do when everybody in the whole world recognizes your superior wisdom and begs you to save them from their own idiocy.

There are only two rules. Rule No. 1, don't hold back. And Rule No. 2, don't put your name on the paper.

When I Become Empress of Everything
Economics:

All jobs that require people to wear paper hats (most of them seem to have to do with serving food, the logic of which escapes me) are abolished. All clocks designed to push people around (alarm clocks, time clocks) become scrap metal.

New Pay Policy: I institute true pay equity. Women will make $100 to $100,000 per hour, depending on the education, skills, talents and other attributes required by their jobs. Men make 59 cents an hour, no matter what they do. This is only fair, because, being unable to bear children, men are incapable of producing their own replacements and are, therefore, of little economic value to society.

New Tax Policy: I institute the following new taxes:

* Fashion Fraud Tax: $50 for each offense, including but not limited to wearing:
  • polo shirts under sports coats,
  • blue jeans with sports coats,
  • athletic shoes with sports coats,
  • bicycling shorts at a gallery opening,
  • a photographer's vest if you're not a photographer,
  • safari clothes in an urban area,
  • military fatigues in a nation at peace,
  • clothing made out of vinyl or other petroleum products

I think this leaves *plenty* of room for self-expression, don't you?

* Olfactory Assault Tax: 50 bucks if I smell you before I see you.

* Noise Tax: $50 for each instance of causing unnecessary, unwanted noise that trespasses on other people's sanity. For example: Pointing stereo speakers towards neighbor's window; honking automobile horn when not in immediate danger of violent death; failing to have

a muffler; playing heavy metal with your windows rolled down in a traffic jam; speaking to people you do not know ("Hey, aren't you Margaux Hemingway?"); any use of a chain saw or lawn mower.

* Ugliness Tax: $500 for each instance of public ugliness, such as strip shopping centers, parking garages, gray snow and industrial waste. They may be unavoidable, but, dammit, somebody's going to pay!

* Stupidity Tax: $5,000 for each act of overt stupidity. A good example of this would be a guy who demonstrates against abortion but fails to pay his child support. Some people are just so stupid they should have to pay the rest of us for putting up with them.

This revenue will allow me to abolish all current taxes and provide free education through the doctoral level for anyone who desires it, as well as a generous wardrobe and entertainment allowance.

Law & Order:

Instead of prisons, we'll have hell. I'll hire Steven Spielberg and Jerry Falwell to make a hell on earth, and I'll tell everybody that if they commit a crime, they go to hell. I think this threat will work better if people know for sure that hell really does exist. They can even visit it. I'll give tours of hell on Sundays, and at the end of the tours I'll say: "Well, there it is. If you want to stay out of hell, forget about sending money to TV evangelists with bad toupees, just don't rape or murder anybody, steal anything, or adopt disgusting personal habits."

Of course, there won't be any capital punishment; criminals will just burn in hell forever.

Human Relations:

People are going to have to start acting like adult human beings. I've had just about all the whiny neuroses I can take. Right now, once and for all, *everybody:* Stop loving too much, get over your fear of commitment, pick a sexual preference you can live with, learn to nurture yourself, manage your stress, enhance your personal reality, make your children shut up, and keep your weird religious ideas to yourself.

Thank you very much.

Human Relations, War Between the Sexes Division: Everybody is tired to death of domestic power struggles and petty arguments. Ending this war is as simple as reminding the citizens of this country that we live in a democracy (except that I have final say in everything), and in a democracy the majority rules. And the majority of people in this country are what? Women. The United States of America is hereby declared a democratic matriarchy where every woman is queen of her castle and caller of the shots.

About Sex: Since I'm the government, it's really none of my business.

Science:

Some scientists say the universe is expanding. Others say it is contracting. They are both right. Here's why: As we all know, the universe began with the Big Bang. As we also know, the result of a Big Bang is — if we are lucky—the Big O, or Cosmic Orgasm. An orgasm is a series of contractions: contract, expand, contract, expand . . . We can expect the universe to fall asleep any minute.

New Frontiers in Technology: Any computer that subjects you to a billing error must pick up your credit card tab for the next year. What good is technology if it doesn't improve the quality of our lives?

Not bad for my first day as Empress, *huh?* I feel better already. Go ahead—show the world what *you* can do.

CANDYCE MEHERANI

The Imperfect Hostess

ROZ CHAST

Memo From the Sick Bed of a Working Mother

Feel lousy. Head three times normal size. Third day out sick. Boss probably thinks, "Ha! A likely story." Should come see. Look in throat. All red. Tongue white. Right eye hardly opens. Temp: 102. Orally. Probably higher other way. Chilled to bone. Why so with temp 102? How come cold when hot? Coughing, hacking, sneezing. Husband no longer sleeping in same bed. Daughter holds nose when comes in with juice or water for dying mother.

Fumble for glass of orange juice on bedside table. Prop self on elbow to drink. Orange juice dribbles down chin, runs down neck, soaks into pajama top. Now all sticky. Should change, but too weak to get up.

Phone rings. Flop to other side of bed to answer. Son calling from college. Tells me eat lots of broccoli and potatoes because high in vitamin C. Ask son if should feed cold or starve fever or other way around. Son doesn't know. Lotta bucks for college and son doesn't know. What education for? Son says read in paper that flu season mild this year. Ha! A likely story. Education for writing lies about flu season.

Daughter turns on loud music in next room. Would yell, "Turn down!" if throat wasn't so sore. Daughter probably listening to "Grateful Dead." Bad music, good title. Would be grateful if group dead. Be grateful if self dead. At least, not sick then.

What thinking? Didn't mean that, God. Do not want to die. Ever. Miss see smart son graduate from college. Miss see husband, daughter, grandchildren. Miss work. If die, Boss probably think, "Ha! A likely story." Boss probably check pulse in casket.

Wonder if should call doctor. Which doctor? Ob/Gyn? Hope not pregnant. Internist? Eye, ear, nose, throat man? All specialize now. Who call when head three times normal size? Look in yellow pages. Let fingers do walking. Forget. Yellow pages too heavy to lift even when well. Anyway, can't find fingers. Have to look in yellow pages for them. Ha, ha, little joke on self. Must feel better if play little joke. Or could be getting delirious.

Would daughter know what to do if find mother delirious? Must. Daughter knows everything. Is seventeen. Remember being seventeen. How long ago? Can no longer subtract. Wonder if brain dead. No surprise to boss.

Remember when little and got sick. Mother fixed mustard plaster. Stinky, but worked. Mother said it drew poison from system. Hate to think of poison in system. Virus better word. Means same thing, but better word. Unless talking about AIDS virus. How know not full of AIDS poison? Once sure not pregnant and was. Maybe AIDS communist plot—germ warfare. Russians put AIDS poison in vodka. Should write novel about that some day. Should write mother first. Should not drink vodka again, ever.

Husband home now. Know because hear classical music. Wonder if husband would know what to do if find me delirious. Probably run around the house like a madman first and then call police. Then call boss. Boss would say, "Ha! A likely story." Would tell husband I always act delirious.

Hear sounds from kitchen as husband and daughter fix dinner. Want to tell them about broccoli and potatoes, but mouth too dry. Nose unplugging, though, and now can smell chicken soup! Hope get some. Chicken soup ancient cure like mustard plaster. Tastes better than broccoli and potatoes, too.

Husband brings dinner tray with chicken soup. After just a few spoonsful, feel better. Head back to normal size. Can breathe. Throat no longer sore. Not worried anymore about having AIDS, being pregnant, becoming delirious or dying. Just worried about work piled up on desk.

Call co-worker to find out how much work piled up on desk. She says not much because boss has called in sick last two days.

Ha!

A likely story!

JEAN JEFFREY GIETZEN

"Oh my God, WE'RE TURNING INTO OUR MOTHERS!"

A.J. TOOS

Something To Do

One morning I wake up bored. I feel too connected to Boston Edison; the phone company; Saks; to the library where I have worked for four years since graduating from college; to friends who depend on me for company and I them; to old lovers wanting to be friends; to my current lover searching for a way gracefully to stop seeing me—as if I didn't know things are over long before they end.

I decide *to lie.*

I call my lover at his office, which automatically limits his responses. I tell him I have found someone else. I have found someone who brushes my long blonde hair, someone who reads as I read instead of pacing till I stop, who cooks elaborate breakfasts while I give myself a pedicure, someone who does not mix his laundry in with mine. My lover is necessarily speechless as I voice some regrets. He hangs up, but I know he is torn between relief and surprise.

This has made me nervous. I always tell the truth and assume others do, too. At times I have felt like the Statue of Liberty, the goddess Athena, Emma Goldman, Queen Victoria, although I don't know what they thought of lying. Perhaps it is the strength of their arms, one always raised on high.

I call my boss at the library and tell him the distant aunt who welcomed me into her spinster home when my parents died in a fiery plane crash, that distant aunt is ill and asking for me in New Orleans where I grew up. (It is a place I have always wanted to go.) I tell him I might be gone two weeks, that I won't know the length of my stay until I have consulted her doctor. I mention her quavering voice saying her paid companion of the past twelve years has run off with the silver and the handyman. I am expected to search for both. I will humor her, I tell my boss, but I am really going in order to be near her when she dies. The last word makes him shy so he says he will wait to hear from me. I ask that my current project be put aside, my papers put in a drawer, that it is something I'd prefer to finish myself. I can't really remember what is on my desk besides the clear nail polish I wish I now had.

As I am making myself a cup of strong tea someone calls and asks for "George." This time I do not apologize for the caller's mistake. It is a woman's voice and it seems surprised by my own. I tell her George is in the shower, that he likes to take long, soapy showers. I take her number, repeat it back to her, but suggest that she call again in an hour.

The phone rings once more. A friend's husband is delighted he's caught me before I've left for work. He invites me to a surprise party for his wife's thirtieth birthday. He explains it will not be tacky. We will not be required to spring from closets or emerge from behind a couch. We will not be led in cheery singing, or shout "surprise." I tell him his taste verges on the profound, that until now no time seemed appropriate for saying so. I picture his bald head, his dome ridged like the one over the statehouse. Bald men have problems women cannot assuage. When he invites me to lunch later in the week, I accept. I name a tiny French restaurant, cozy, expensive, and so romantically lit I feel sure he will be unable to find me there. He breathes deeply, says good-bye. One always has friends one dislikes.

My best friend calls. (Not the wife of the surprise party.) She also works at the library. I take the phone and my tea into the bedroom and get comfortable. My stomach feels tight from the tension of my lies. My friend has heard "the story" about my aunt from our boss. She says "the story" because she thinks she recognizes a lie when she hears one. *Maybe.* I tell her I tried calling her last night. I say last week there had seemed no need to relay my worst fears to her. But now that they are realized, now that I am pregnant—I hesitate and sip my tea, allowing her to say a few nonjudgmental but soothing words of support to the effect that whatever I do she will understand. I tell her my lover and I are taking a trip that will include an abortion. It will be a bond between us, perhaps leading to the marriage I have longed for. I am annoyed that she swallows this last remark. I hold white lingerie up to my breasts and imagine an unusual wedding.

I immediately call my father to set things right. He is surprised to hear from me in daytime hours, the rates between Ohio and Boston being what they are. He says he's just about to go to the Elks for some poker. Looking out over the faces at my mother's funeral I realized that the Elks had won. He says the raccoons kept him awake all night and now what? Why Dad, I tell him, I'm just calling to say hello. (I never call to say hello.) His deeply suspicious nature is unable to relax into small talk, so I am forced to admit reluctantly the true reason for my call. I am annoyed by his sudden intake of breath, his certainty that I haven't failed him yet. He has already constructed various scenarios for me. He suspects I live my life to embarrass him in front of his friends. How can I disappoint him? I tell him I've decided to keep the child. "What child?" does not occur to him. The child he has been prepared for—notwithstanding that I was probably the first valedictorian of my town to hold forth on birth control at slumber parties. I say, "You'd better sit down before I tell you about the father." I hear the kitchen chair being scraped across to the wall phone by the refrigerator. I tell him we have decided not to marry, that our relationship has been ending anyway. I imagine him only half listening, already rehearsing his role in the tragedy when I arrive home on the train (he's never flown), a wet bundle in my arms.

He asks who is the father—his voice dreading the wrong race or color. That the father is unsuitable goes without saying. I feel him hoping the father is merely a married man, or an inmate of the minimum security prison he warned me against teaching furniture refinishing at, or that the father is an intelligent priest I have temporarily led astray. I announce that my lover is eschewing all legal rights to the child. I rephrase this to eliminate eschew. I say that he has decided to return to the Punjab (let him look it up) and I am taking a two-week vacation to see him off. I tell my father I love him, wishing I did. The most he'll lose today is five or ten dollars. At the Elks the stakes aren't high.

My lover calls back as I am cleaning out the refrigerator, snacking on leftovers. Now he is huddled in a phone booth trying to talk above the noise of trucks going by, and full of questions too indiscreet to utter in his office. He wants to see me but I tell him I'm not well. There is a red mold on the green beans that is the brightest I've ever seen. He demands to see me, he will be over in half an hour, but I mention I changed my locks last week when my purse was stolen on the subway. He doesn't remember my telling him this. Surely I would have told him of such a terrible thing. Perhaps this accounts . . . I cut him off lamenting his faulty memory. "Who?" he asks. "Is it someone I know?" I realize he is behaving exactly as I might had our places been reversed. He is behaving badly. This time I hang up, tempted to tell tales of pregnancy, but I refrain.

I do not call my sister in New York. She'll be hearing from our father tonight at 11:01. I'm grateful for the ten-hour reprieve. I'll send her the first postcard. The possibilities are endless as I locate my colored pens.

My landlady beams. She promises to water the plants, which I have gathered together in my bay window, to take in my mail. She is so excited for me she wrings her hands in blessing. I'm the first person she knows to actually win something big like a trip, though her cousin used to enter all the contests and wrote jingles that were pure poetry.

I call to cancel my subscription to *Library Journal.* I tell them that some how their computer has been sending me seventeen issues for the past three months. No doubt it is happening to others. I refrain from telling them of the new efficient filing system I have quietly instituted in the reference section of my library.

My next-door neighbor watches me pack after making us both Bloody Marys. She is sympathetic, though surprised, at my career change. She never *could* picture me a librarian, what with no glasses, all that blonde hair. She didn't know that Arizona State had the best veterinary school in the country. Wasn't it all snakes and bears in that area? Animals not in need of medicine? I magnanimously wave aside her lack of knowledge and show her a picture of my childhood cat. It is a photo I found last week marking someone's place in *The Annals of European Civilization.* As I fold clothes I tell her how "David Livingstone" got her name. She turns the photo over and reads "Muffy." Oh, only my crazy aunt called her that, I say.

"Getting married in New Orleans." My travel agent smiles widely. "How absolutely romantic." I mention my hesitation at meeting his parents. They are one of the prominent families always to be found at the head of the Mardi Gras parade. They live in a grand home in the disintegrating Garden District and are probably disappointed in what they've heard of me. "Not you," she says, "you'll knock them dead." I promise to try.

On the way to the airport, my cab driver practices for the Indianapolis 500. I tell him I feel queasy, that perhaps he should slow down, I hope I make it to a restroom. His foot jumps from the gas and he cleaves to the slow lane. "Hey, Lady, just hold on. I have another six hours' work tonight," he says, glancing back at me. I relax and promise to mention him in my prayers that evening in Paris.

Finally, fifteen minutes before boarding time, I call the police, handkerchief over the phone. I explain slowly and carefully about the bombs I have placed in the Public Library. I say I have had a change of heart—they have a fighting chance with early warning. (These threats are always good for at least a half-hour coffee break.) I try to think of a signature to tip off my friends working there, to make them suspiciously thankful, but I don't want to stay on the phone. Begin in Fiction I say.

The plane seems to be waiting for me. The hostess smiles like one of my detested sorority sisters but I ignore her and incline my head to the handsome silly pilot. The gentleman dressed like a banker is sympathetic to my claustrophobia and graciously offers his window seat. I settle back remembering the day.

PAMELA PAINTER

Philosophy of Life

I have so much to do
I can't possibly get it done so
I'm not going to start.

CHOCOLATE WATERS

CHILDREN: PRO OR CON

GAMES TO PLAY
WITH KIDS

IN

THE CAR

"Churchmouse" ~
First one who makes
the slightest peep loses.

"Telepathy" ~
Everybody tries to send
their thoughts to every-
body else without speaking.

"Foxhole" ~
Children pretend that they
are in a foxhole on a
battlefield and therefore
must not utter a sound.

ROZ CHAST

Children: Pro or Con?

Moving, as I do, in what would kindly be called artistic circles, children are an infrequent occurrence. But even the most artistic of circles includes within its periphery a limited edition of the tenaciously domestic.

As I am generally quite fond of children I accept this condition with far less displeasure than do my more rarefied acquaintances. That is not to imply that I am a total fool for a little grin but simply that I consider myself to be in a position of unquestionable objectivity and therefore eminently qualified to deal with the subject in an authoritative manner.

From the number of children in evidence it appears that people have them at the drop of a hat — for surely were they to give this matter its due attention they would act with greater decorum. Of course, until now prospective parents have not had the opportunity to see the facts spelled out in black and white and therefore cannot reasonably be held accountable for their actions. To this end I have carefully set down all pertinent information in the fervent hope that it will result in a future populated by a more attractive array of children than I have thus far encountered.

Pro

I must take issue with the term "a mere child," for it has been my invariable experience that the company of a mere child is infinitely preferable to that of a mere adult.

Children are usually small in stature, which makes them quite useful for getting at those hard-to-reach places.

Children do not sit next to one in restaurants and discuss their preposterous hopes for the future in loud tones of voice.

Children ask better questions than do adults. "May I have a cookie?" "Why is the sky blue?" and "What does a cow say?" are far more likely to elicit a cheerful response than "Where's your manuscript?" "Why haven't you called?" and "Who's your lawyer?"

Children give life to the concept of immaturity.

Children make the most desirable opponents in Scrabble as they are both easy to beat and fun to cheat.

It is still quite possible to stand in a throng of children without once detecting even the faintest whiff of an exciting, rugged after-shave or cologne.

Not a single member of the under-age set has yet to propose the word *chairchild.*

Children sleep either alone or with small toy animals. The wisdom of such behavior is unquestionable, as it frees them from the immeasurable tedium of being privy to the whispered confessions of others. I have yet to run across a teddy bear who was harboring the secret desire to wear a maid's uniform.

Con

Even when freshly washed and relieved of all obvious confections, children tend to be sticky. One can only assume that this has something to do with not smoking enough.

Children have decidedly little fashion sense and if left to their own devices will more often than not be drawn to garments of unfortunate cut. In this respect they do not differ greatly from the majority of their elders, but somehow one blames them more.

Children respond inadequately to sardonic humor and veiled threats.

Notoriously insensitive to subtle shifts in mood, children will persist in discussing the color of a recently sighted cement-mixer long after one's own interest in the topic has waned.

Children are rarely in the position to lend one a truly interesting sum of money. There are, however, exceptions, and such children are an excellent addition to any party.

Children arise at an unseemly hour and are ofttimes in the habit of putting food on an empty stomach.

Children do not look well in evening clothes.

All too often children are accompanied by adults.

FRAN LEBOWITZ

Everyone Says Babies
Are Difficult

Everyone says babies are difficult; it's just not true. Changing diapers, wiping pabulum from chins, heating bottles in the middle of the night are a snap compared to picking up your own telephone that you pay for every month and never hearing a familiar voice, either friend or relative, but rather a barbarian girl or boy demanding, "Tom home!" I was at first annoyed by the question and then by the tone, but I've trained myself to respond only to the question asked: "Why, yes, he is. How kind of you to call and inquire. I must go now." I then hang up. The barbarian response next was, "Can I speak to Tom?" to which I replied, again, as sweetly as possible: "It appears you are quite capable. I hear you very well. I must go now." Finally they reached the desired question: "May I speak to Tom?" which, unfortunately, elicits "I'm sorry, dear, but Thomas may not use the telephone until his grades improve." I don't add "Or hell freezes over."

Whichever comes first. Hell will surely win.

NIKKI GIOVANNI
(excerpt from *Sacred Cows . . . and Other Edibles*)

BABY TALK

CONTINUES NEXT PAGE . . .

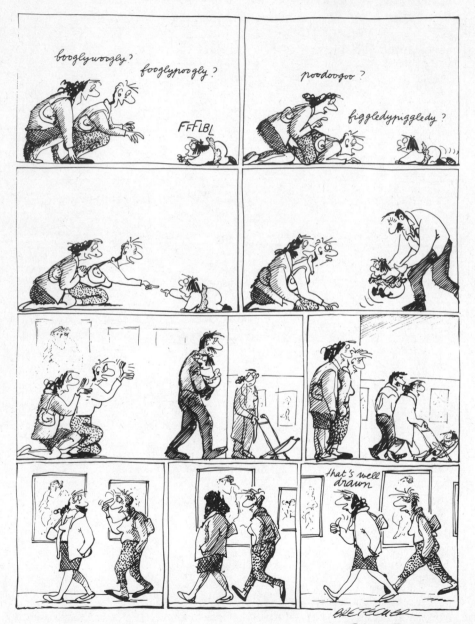

CLAIRE BRETECHER

Baby Burnout

Two nannies stroll two babies out of the Guggenheim, where "The Sophia Parker-Stuart Retrospective: 1984-1989" is on exhibit.

Baby 1
What did you think?
Baby 2
I think she peaked at 22 months with her fingerpaint series.
Baby 1
But didn't you love the collages? I thought they had so much charm. You rarely see such naivete in the work of a three year old today.
Baby 2
Chacun son gout.
Baby 1
You and your nanny want to stop for an apple juice somewhere?
Baby 2
Can't. I have Ballet Babies at 11, then Tennis for Tots, Japanese tutorial, Lollipop Choir, and Playskool.
Baby 1
Aren't you a little old for Playskool?
Baby 2
I'm a board of trustee.
Baby 1
Oh. Where will you be at 5?
Baby 2
SAT prep. Where I am going to be in big trouble.
Baby 1
Why?
Baby 2
Didn't do the homework. My computer broke last night.
Baby 1
That's the pits.
Baby 2
Two chapters of my novel erased! My therapist says I *wanted* the chapters erased but . . .
Baby 1
You didn't tell me you were writing a novel.
Baby 2
Memoirs actually; focusing on the early part of my life. It's stream of conscious, because I started writing it before I knew how to talk. Should I send you a manuscript?

Baby 1

My fax number is 35447683. Speaking of numbers, did you see Sesame Street this morning?

Baby 2

No. I find that show so didactic. Besides, I have my power nap then.

Baby 1

Boy, I could use a nap right now.

Baby 2

Or a vacation. I'd like to just lie somewhere in a playpen with a good picture book.

Baby 1

Or a rattle. Remember rattles?

Baby 2

Yeah. And kangarockaroos?

Baby 1

And snugglies?

Baby 2

Oh, snugglies . . .

BABIES FALL ASLEEP.

Nanny 1

I can't believe he left you for *her!*

Nanny 2

He said he loved me, but he didn't find me fun anymore. He said the child in me had died.

Nanny 1

That's ridiculous!

Nanny 2

I said we could go to a play counselor, we could *learn* to play, but he said . . .

PATRICIA MARX

CONTEMPORARY LIFE

NICOLE HOLLANDER

The Magic Kingdom

Before I went to Disney World, my major cultural compromise was the percentage of polyester in my sweat pants. I've worked in natural food stores since they were invented, back in the days when we wore long cotton skirts for everything except cross-country skiing. I drive a rattle-trap car, and for years I refused to use paper towels, aluminum foil, or plastic bags, much to my mother's annoyance.

Most of the wheatberry mentality stayed with me through the high-tech, me-first onslaught of the '80's. But I was given a ticket to go to Disney World for a family reunion. The monorail drove through the lobby of our hotel, Goofy sat down and had breakfast with us, and the Polynesian dancers had grass skirts made of mylar. The last day there, we went for a boat ride down the confluence of the Amazon, Congo, and Ganges Rivers. The captain shrieked, "Watch out!" as we skirted plastic computerized alligators. He extolled the splendors of fiberglass giraffes, and made mother-in-law jokes about the mechanical monkeys. When we got back to the quai, I noticed that the pilings, which looked like rotting wood, were Dow Chemical right to their little inorganic heartwoods. I reached some kind of critical mass.

"What kind of anthropomorphic arrogance is this?" I screamed, refusing to get off the boat. "What are you teaching our children? That it's possible to invent an improved giraffe? And what's *that*?" I jumped up on the seat and pointed at the quai. "That's a LIE. You're LYING to our CHILDREN." The crowd waiting to board was interested. They'd been in line for an hour and ten minutes, and this was a diversion. The captain and his dock crew were less amused.

"Everything's going to be all right," they hissed. "We'll help you to a place out of the sun. You'll feel better."

"It's not the sun," I spat at them. "And don't come one step further, or I'll jump overboard and get a concussion on an alligator."

I shouted over their heads at the crowd, "Don't take this ride! Your children's psyches will never recover. Take them to the zoo. Or save the millions it costs to come here and go to Brazil. *Or* Africa. *Or* India." I saw a worker sliding along the rail to my right. I swung one leg over the rail. He stopped. "Or read a book. Remember them? Walt Disney didn't mean for us to make the world into a cartoon. Stay away from here until they agree to have *real* rotting pilings."

The captain was moving toward me again. "Why don't we go talk this over?" he said with a condescension usually reserved for nursing home patients.

"Don't talk to me like that, twerp. I was at Columbia in '68, when you were being potty-trained. You don't scare me at all. Watch." And I swung my other leg over the rail and dropped into the Amazon-Congo-Ganges. Up to my waist. I waded around the boat so the crowd could see me. "Look, kids! This big river is waist deep!" I splashed over to the nearest alligator and patted it on the nose. "These people think you kids are stupid. ARE YOU?"

"No!" screamed back a handful of kids who were getting into the spirit.

"Wouldn't you rather see *real* alligators?"

"YES!" The chorus was growing.

I could tell the captain was resigning himself to getting his uniform dirty. He was taking off his shoes.

"There's plenty of *really* miraculous stuff out there, kids. Look at the birds and the flowers." I'd clambered up on the alligator's back and was riding it like a surfboard. "Don't let grown-ups impose these industrialized fantasies on you. Let your *own* imaginations soar!" I reached up into the sky to demonstrate the limitless possibilities.

A number of the parents were beginning to look annoyed. The captain and two dock workers were wading toward me. The captain held his hands up to protect his hair from splashes.

"Who's that woman?" I heard a little kid ask.

"Just some crazy lady, dear." soothed her mother.

"I'm *not* a crazy lady. These people are." I pointed to the captain. "This whole place is." I swung my arm at the Magic Kingdom. And I slipped off the alligator with a great splash. A cheer went up from the crowd. The captain moved in for the kill; when I resurfaced, he grabbed me and dragged me, sodden cotton skirt and all, to a ladder up the infamous pilings of the high-tech resin quai. I could see my sister on shore assuring a security guard that I was harmless.

"The real thing is more than Coca-Cola, kids!" I screamed. "Don't let these dodos insult your intelligence! Tell them you want a *real* alligator!"

"A real alligator would've eaten you up!" someone shouted from the crowd.

I could tell the captain wished he had thought of that.

I laughed. "I would have shown a real alligator more respect!"

My sister was saying, "She has these spells when she forgets her medication." She took my arm and waved what looked like her birth-control pills in front of the guard's face. "Now show us a drinking fountain, and she'll be fine in no time."

"At least his hairdo's messed up," I called to the crowd. Then I added conversationally, "Abbie Hoffman never used mousse, you know." I looked at the captain. "So what's wrong with Sea World? Can't they loan you some real animals?"

"Can't the Grand Canyon loan us some real tourists?" one of the dock workers said under his breath.

The captain leaned back and crossed his arms over his chest.

My sister was pulling me toward the exit. "By the way," I called back, "your fly is down. Mechanized fiberglass in there, too?"

TAFFY FIELD

Change In the Weather

(a hymn of gratitude to the National Oceanic and Atmospheric Administration on the occasion of their decision to name some Pacific storms after men)

Good news from the meteorological front!
Now half of our storms will be manly and blunt,
Objective, broad shouldered, and legally free
From female caprices and hyperbole.

Amelia and Bess must yield some of their hail
And their showers and tempests and squalls to the male.
Carlotta and Rosa will find that a breeze
Can whisper Vicente as well as Louise.

Who wouldn't feel snug in the eye of a storm
Called Daniel or Sergio or Hector or Norm?
And surely we'll all sleep more easily nights
Since weather, at least, has achieved equal rights.

MARY HAZZARD

KNOWING things

· L Y N D A · B A R R Y · © 1 9 8 9

MY SISTER MARLYS IS DOING A PROJECT OUT ON THE BACK PORCH ABOUT PLANTS. SHES ONLY 8 SO SHE'S STILL NOT SICK OF KNOWING THINGS. I DID THAT SAME PROJECT ABOUT A MILLION YEARS AGO. YOU PLANT BEANS IN A MILK CARTON. BIG DEAL.

I TOLD HER SHE ONLY NEEDS THREE TO DO THE EXPERIMENT OF ① NO WATER. ② SOME WATER. ③ FLOODING. SHE PLANTED 30. SHE'S TRYING KOOLAID, MILK, AND CRAGMONT ROOT BEER. SHE RUBBED ONE WITH VICKS. SHE PUT MILK DUDS IN THE DIRT OF ONE. SHE SAYS SHE'S LOOKING FOR THE SECRET FORMULA.

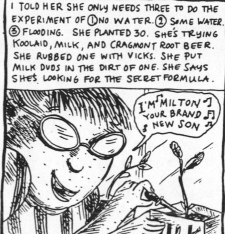

WHEN I TRY TO TELL HER THERE'S NO WAY, SHE GOES: "THAT'S WHAT THEY ALL SAY." I DON'T KNOW WHERE SHE EVEN GOT THAT! IT'S FROM THE BOOKS YOU KEEP READING WITH NO REALITY IN THEM. A MAGIC TREE STARTS TALKING OR A MAGIC DOG STARTS TALKING AND EVERYTHING IN THE WORLD CAN BE MAGIC. EVEN YOUR SPIT CAN BE MAGIC. AND NOW THAT'S WHAT SHE THINKS. THERE'S ONE PLANT SHE SPITS ON.

I TRIED TO EXPLAIN TO HER THE CONCEPT OF REALITY AND THAT REALITY IS BEAUTIFUL. AND SHE SAID HER PLANTS WERE REALITY AND SHE WAS REALITY AND HER EXPERIMENTS WERE REALITY AND I SAID THE REAL REALITY WAS SHE WAS THE TORTURER OF PLANTS AND ALL THE PLANTS WERE GOING TO DIE BECAUSE OF HER AND WHAT I SAID CAME TRUE. IT CAME TRUE. IT CAME TRUE. MARLYS, I'M SORRY IT CAME TRUE.

LYNDA BARRY

In Praise of Motor Boats

The other day I'm sitting on the rickety porch of a friend's camp on the edge of a small lake, about 3 miles long. A sublime summer day—sunshine, the fresh green, birdsong, a pot of tea, talk of the world's troubles, and all that. Pretty soon we hear the raw/raw/raw of a motor starting up and, soon after that, a motor boat about the size of half a city block blasts by dragging a single water skier. Just before the first wake hits the shore, the boat is back, then it turns and is back, and it goes back and forth, back and forth, and I thought well, how wonderful.

Summer is so boring. I mean we were exhausted with the peace and quiet, our companionship, the reiteration of birdsong, the talk of the world, anyhow. A good thing we were, because now we could no longer hear each other, much less the boring birds. So I decided then and there to write a modest essay in praise of the 123,723 motor boats registered in Maine as of December 1, 1988. I'd like to include some praise of the motor boats towed up here for the summer from out-of-state, too. The 123,723 doesn't include out-of-state boats, if those boats are registered elsewhere and enjoy Maine waters for less than 60 peaceful summer days. I tried to find out, so that they could get their share of praise, too, but no office, bureau, or whatever has any idea how many out-of-state boats join the in-state fleet of 123,723. The rough guess is many thousands more.

Nevertheless, we can safely assume, I should think, that the thousands of boats towed up here from away exhibit the same virtues as the 123,723 already registered in Maine. And we can also rest assured that Maine's approximately 96 full-time Game Wardens and 28 part-time "assistant" wardens (under whose joint jurisdiction fall all "recreational vehicles" now: snowmobiles, dirt bikes, ATV's, plus nerdy non-motorized boats like canoes, sailboats, dinghies, etc., plus the 123,723 in-state motor boats, as well as however many thousand out-of-state motor boats) have an easy, laid-back job taking care of the maybe 1 or 2 boating violations that occur over the summer in Vacationland. I mean, I think we have plenty of supervision here, don't you? For example, there are 4 full-time Wardens right in our area, responsible for 42 towns in 3 counties with 105 lakes and ponds, not counting rivers. And I mean these Wardens are well paid. You would not believe the salary they draw for just driving around in the nice fishing season, the peaceful summertime, the picturesque hunting season, and so forth. So there's a poacher once in a while, or a nut driving his truck out on thin ice, or a drunk on jet skis once in a blue moon. Giving the Wardens a little extra work — responsibility for 123,723 motor boats plus however many more from out-of-state, hey—they're getting paid, right?

Okay. So here's my list of what's wonderful about motor boats. Space is limited, and it's hard to know where to stop, so I'll just say—Dear Reader, feel free to add your own praises, too; I'm sure I've left out some important things.

1. **Motorboats Are Popular.** Does right make might, or might make right? I forget, but either way, think about this: the population of Maine is around 1,125,000. That means (123,723 motorboats) roughly 1 motorboat per 10 people. Now commercial craft, like fishing boats, aside, this figure has to say something. If almost everybody loves malls, loves development, thinks the Maine Turnpike should be widened to accommodate tourists, doesn't that sort of consensus make you feel left out, as if there's something wrong with you? It should. Even President Bush has a motorboat. Maybe more than one. So, if you're opposed to 123,723 motorboats, including the President's, because you like peace and quiet, or you like to fish from the bank, or go out in a canoe or sailboat or a little fishing boat at dusk, with a like-zero horsepower putt-putt motor on back, or you like loons, or you have quirky environmental concerns like the "greenhouse effect" (which is probably just a scare tactic anyhow), try to get with it, won't you?

2. **123,723 Motorboats Give Maine a Better Self Image.** So everyone thinks we're poor up here, that we all live like the Beans of Egypt. Well this proves we don't. We have bucks. For example, the popular 130 horsepower Stern Drive Crestliner goes 45 mph, comes with "plenty of plush pile carpeting and contour-padded seating," is $11,500, up front. Sea-Doo, a "personal watercraft with a real edge," 40 mph, a "fantastic ride," subject of a recent article, "Getting It Up," in the latest issue of the personal watercraft mag., is only $4,400 and, at that price, we'll be wanting one for every member of the family. Or just go ahead and get that Family Boat you've been dreaming about: the 454 King Cobra, 350 horsepower, a great little lake boat, goes 70 mph, $24,000, not including financing. Facts like these make us proud. Who says us Mainers can't have good, clean fun—and pay for it, too?

3. **Motorboats Are Good Clean Fun.** Oh all right, they cause some dirt now and then, like air and water pollution, eye/ear/nose/brain pollution, shoreline erosion, the litter of floating feathers and dead fish; or folks throw their styrofoam, Pampers, six-pack rings and butts overboard; or flush their boat potties into Sebago, and other mischievous doings. But basically, boating is Clean: the pile carpeting stays clean, the contour-padded seats stay clean, the Wife and Kiddies and Clients stay clean, the cooler, the chips, the towels stay clean, and so on.

4. **Motorboats Get You Back to Nature.** Say you've got a lake 5 miles long and a boat that'll average 50 miles per hour. This means you can make roughly 10 trips an hour, or, one trip every 6 minutes. There's

just no estimating how much of God's great world you can take in at that speed.

    5. Motorboats Help the General Economy. Budweiser, Coors, Pepsi, Coke, Exxon, Frito-Lay, Coppertone, and many, many more. To say nothing of Honda, Suzuki, Tohatsu, Yamaha, Nissan, Kawsaki, and other corporations dedicated to building and maintaining a free America at play, self-supporting and independent.

    6. Motorboats Help with the Ongoing Need for the Conquest of Nature. Now this may seem contradictory but, when you Get Back To It (see #4 above) you realize that Nature has to be kept at bay. This effort should never slack off, otherwise cuckoos, whippoorwills, loons, bass, salmon, blue herons, puffins, and other rampaging examples of Nature red in tooth and claw like ferns, mosses, duck eggs and violent stuff like that, might take over. And where would we be then? Motorboating, especially of the back and forth, back and forth all afternoon sort, leaves man's mark, makes an impact on the environment, probably a lasting one. That keeps Nature under control, and shows who's who, and thus is related (see #2 above) to a healthy Self Image. Especially when you multiply that by 123,723, plus whatever comes in from out-of-state.

    7. Motorboats Make Us Free. Free to enjoy ourselves, free to express ourselves, free to spend our own money the way we want to spend it, free to assert our rights, free to annoy, spoil, drive bonkers, wreck, ruin, pollute, free to be tearin' up the lake like a big old dinosaur. Plus, the Law, for once, is on Our Side. It makes sure we are Free to do all the above and more. God bless America, is what I say.

    8. The Law—Such As It Is—Is On Our Side, for Once. A law? Don't worry: not much of a law. There is no law that protects anything about the non-human or human *environment*. No law, for example, about how fast you can go or how much noise your Cobra makes, or your Cigarette boat, or your Sea-Doo. There's a law about "safety," and one, I think, about "harassment." That means somebody has to be there and actually see us veering too close to Camp Lose-A-Leg, endangering the Little Nippers bodily; or somebody has to catch us deliberately chasing Mother Loon and Babies. And then they have to call — no, not the State Police, not their problem, but the Warden — who will then, if they can find him, and as soon as he can get the time, come out and chug after us in his probably about 15 horsepower boat, if that, hours later. And if and when he finds us, he can tap us on the wrist a bit, read us a wimp of a riot act, give us a fine. Other than that, motorboating on Maine lakes is what our Forefathers fought the 4th of July about. Fish, loons, somebody who wants to canoe or watch the sunset or read on his porch, that's not what the Revolution was about. Local control? Locals making claims that we're wrecking their lake, their lives? Don't worry; Be Happy. The town the lake is in, or the folks along the edge, they're powerless. Because the

State owns the water, the State won't let towns or lake associations make their own laws; and the State has no laws itself; and even if it did, what can 96 Game Wardens do? So relax. The Water, like all Good Things, except King Cobras, is just about Free.

Go for it.

ALICE BLOOM

Epigram for the Educational Testing Service

So much depends
upon

a small blue
rectangle

filled in with
pencil

scanned by giant
computers.

JANET RUTH HELLER

MARIAN HENLEY

The Van

Chevy van, who made thee?
Dost thou know who made thee?
Gave thee pointed mouse-like nose,
Painted thee metallic rose;
Gave thee airbags puffing out,
And stereo speakers all about;
Gave thee tinted window glass,
And heated seats to warm one's ass!
Yuppie van who made thee?
Dost thou know who made thee?

Chevy van I'll tell thee
Yuppie van I'll tell thee!
The man who makes the megabuck,
While General Motors runs amuck:
He hands out pink slips with each pay,
This corporate king of Chevrolet:
He doesn't give a flying fuck,
When profit's down, you're out—tough luck.
Roger Smith, he made thee.
A piece of shit he made thee.

DEBRA HOFFMAN DECKER

Nurturing Inner-Suspicion

There's a new threat to those of us living in progressive cities and it isn't drug wars, crumbling infra-structures or hazardous waste. The threat I'm talking about is Adult Education.

Let's face it. Adult Education is everywhere and it's getting worse. Times used to be that Adult Ed. meant an innocent water color class or "Refinishing Furniture for Beginners," courses taught through the local high school. Not so anymore. These days anyone can be a teacher. And anyone with a computer can throw together a course catalog. It's a deadly combination.

The worst offenders in the Adult Education field are the self-improvement, easy-therapy type catalogs. Now, don't get me wrong—I'm not an advocate of the AMA or the psychiatrist's couch. I've been massaged and Rolfed. I've been empowered through self-defense classes and feminist psychotherapy. I even have my energy-field cleared periodically. However, as I flip through these "instant therapy" catalogs, my bewilderment grows and my trust level slips.

As I see it, there are three classifications of classes or workshops that qualify for my "Get Real" award. The first is the workshop that promises everything in three hours. Their descriptions usually read something like this:

SELF-LOVE: Enhance your Personal, Sexual, Social, Spiritual and Financial Life and Lose Weight While Doing It.
This workshop builds self-esteem through the power of orgasmic energy and the psychic decision-making process. While reducing anxiety over food and food-related issues, we will explore the spiritual rewards of positive cash-flow and resolve the conflicts of living in the nuclear age. Self-empowerment, self-image, self-awareness, self-growth—do it all while strengthening your personal boundaries. Wear comfortable clothing.

Then there are the instructors who have fallen prey to the "buzzword" sensation. They focus in on—and take advantage of—whatever problem is currently in vogue. Concerned that you can't figure out what the workshop is actually about? Don't worry, the instructor probably doesn't know either. Here's a typical listing:

Heal and reconnect with the cosmic anger of your co-dependant inner child through visualization, dreamwork and meditation. Make life-positive, pro-active choices by repatterning unhealthy and addictive dysfunctional operational modes. Through the intimate process of re-birthing in pairs, rebuild a loving relationship with your ex-husband, no matter what kind of jerk he's been. Discover your inner goddess, unleash your sacred fire, contemplate planetary transmutation. Bring a bag lunch.

And finally, there's the workshops that just can't be classified, that go beyond belief, on this or any other plane of existence. This one is taught through the Parks and Recreation Center of a city which will remain nameless.

The Scarf Encounter

Do you wistfully pass the scarf counter, wishing you knew how to accessorize with lovely silk squares and charming challis scarves? Here's your chance to learn all about scarf tying and how to turn that basic suit or dress into a fantastic, versatile addition to your wardrobe. Learn to emphasize the classic, dramatic or romantic aspects of how you like to dress. Bring three scarves from your wardrobe to class.

I often wonder what the next stage will be. Choosing a pre-school for your inner child? Accessorizing your chakras? Perhaps herbal remedies for your personal computer. Or, maybe, Creative Detachment for a More Peaceful Existence. Creative Detachment . . . wait a minute folks, I think we have a new threat on our hands.

ELLEN ORLEANS

Man Bigot

The man who is a bigot
is the worst thing God has got,
except his match, his woman,
who really is Ms. Begot.

MAYA ANGELOU

N. Leigh Dunlap

DEATH —
THE LAST LAUGH

BRUSH WITH DEATH ON VACATION.

JENNIFER BERMAN

Poem

Because I could not stop for death
It kindly stopped for me —
Its subway rattled to my door
And I got on for free.

LORRAINE SCHEIN

On My Honor

"Carol, why don't you take your Girl Scouts to the mortuary?" Dorothy Claiborne boomed across the produce counter.

"The mortuary?"

"Yes," she continued, "the mortuary gives you a dollar for every person you take to hear their educational public relations program. They'll show you the embalming room and the casket selection. It only takes an hour and on the way out, everyone receives a bottle of hand lotion."

"Really," I said, thinking what a crazy idea it was.

However, we only had two years before our camping trip to Hawaii. We were behind on our money earning, so I thought over her proposal as I continued my marketing.

I ran into Dorothy again in the check-out line. Looking around to make sure no one was listening I lowered my voice and said, "I've been thinking about your suggestion. If each girl took five guests, we could make $150."

"And they'll learn something," Mrs. Claiborne responded as loudly as ever.

"I'll present the idea to the troop next week."

When I told the thirteen year olds about it and they roared with laughter for twenty minutes. However, the vote was unanimous. We would go to the mortuary.

That evening I prepared the parents' permission slip. Then it occurred to me that the mothers and fathers might think that this could be a morbid experience. So, as an afterthought, I wrote across the bottom, in inch-high capital letters: NO DEAD BODIES WILL BE SEEN.

I took my original to the copier and the next week just before the meeting I picked up the duplicates.

"Please, girls," I said to the troop, "be sure your parents and guests understand that this will not be depressing. Notice that I have written, NO DEAD BODIES WILL BE SEEN, on the permission slips."

Marlana immediately began waving her permission slip. "Yes, Marlana, what is it?"

Jumping to her feet she burst out, "Mine says ten dead bodies will be seen!"

I couldn't believe it, but there it was. The original had slipped on the copy machine and the first vertical and diagonal line of the NO had been obliterated. The message clearly read in inch-high capital letters: "10 DEAD BODIES WILL BE SEEN."

"Girls," I asked, "would you please correct your permission slips?"

When I arrived home, my phone was ringing. Before I got the receiver to my ear I heard an angry voice scream, "Wouldn't one dead body be enough?"

Obviously the corrections were never completed. That was years ago, but I can still hear my phone ringing over and over.

This project was a success as a money-earner, though. We repeated it several times, of course being very careful to proofread the permission slips. And, no dead bodies were ever seen.

CAROL L. SIBLEY

NICOLE HOLLANDER

My Mother's Hospital Room Had A View of the East River

My mother's hospital room had a view of the East River. She lay there slowly dying, with my father impatiently standing by. "Pull the plug," he would say to the doctors, and the doctors would calmly explain that there was no plug, there was just the wasting away of life. A few of her former clients came to see her—the scar faces frightened the nurses and the midgets made whoopee on the electric wheelchairs— and now and then she came into focus and made deals. "I think we can get you a hundred thou on the next one," she would say; she hadn't handled a client in years, but she went rattling on about points and box office and below the line and above the line. The nurse would bring lunch. "I think I'll take it in the commissary," she'd say. One day my father called and said, "You'd better come. I think this is it." Of course, he telephoned every day and said that, but it always sounded like wishful thinking; now, finally, I knew he must be right. I went straight to the hospital, and when I went into her room she was sleeping. Suddenly she opened her eyes and looked at me. "I just screwed Darryl Zanuck on the remake," she said, and gave a little croak, which I didn't know at the moment was a significant thing, the actual croak—I thought it was just her gravelly laugh—and died.

"Mother's gone," said the nurse. Not "Your mother" but "Mother." I stared at the nurse, stunned not so much by my mother's death, which after all had been promised for months and, as far as my father was concerned, was long overdue, but by the nurse's presumption. "You can call your mother Mother," I snapped, "but you can't call my mother Mother." The nurse gave me one of those withering looks that are meant to make you feel as if your thoroughly understandable rage is mere female hysteria. She pulled the sheet over my mother's face. "We're going to take Mother away now," she said in a tone so condescending that I became even more wild with anger. "She's not your mother," I shouted. "On top of which she's not gone, she's dead. Do you hear me? *Dead.* And what you're going to take away is her body, so call it a body. Call it a corpse, for Christ's sake." The nurse was now looking at me with an expression of complete horror, which I thought at the time was on account of my behavior, but it wasn't really; it was complete horror at what was happening behind me, which was that my mother had chosen that moment to make a full recovery. The sheet began rising like a slow-motion poltergeist, and then, in a burst, my mother whipped off the cloth and shouted: "Ta da!" Then she fainted. "Fainted dead away" is what the nurse said, which just goes to show you another anomaly of hospital life, which that they only use the word "dead" when it doesn't apply.

"We thought you were dead," I said a few minutes later, when my mother came to.

"I was," she said, "I was." She shook her head slightly, as if trying to remember a fuzzy dream. "I floated away in a white organdy dress and black patent-leather Mary Janes," she said. "I looked like Baby Snooks. I tried to get something to wear that was more dignified, but the dignified clothes were being used on another set." She nodded, it was all coming back now. "I looked down, and there was your father, clicking a clapboard that read: 'Bebe's Death, Take One.' The camera started rolling. I was floating further and further away. I was definitely dead. Your father sold the Tampax stock and bought himself a Borsalino hat. 'Print,' he said. 'It's a wrap.'" She began tapping her breastbone defiantly. "*I* was the one who sat next to Bernard Baruch at a dinner party in 1944 and heard him say, 'Buy something people use once and throw away.' *I* was the one who stuck a Tampax into my twat in 1948 and came out of the bathroom and said, 'See if this is traded over the counter.' *I* was the one who made us rich, and now the bastard is going off and spending my money on bimbos while I'm stuck in goyishe heaven in an inappropriate costume. Fuck this, I said to myself, and at that moment I came back."

NORA EPHRON
(from *Heartburn*)

MARIAN HENLEY

GOODNIGHT!

MARIAN HENLEY

Contributors' Notes

MAYA ANGELOU is the author of the best-selling *I Know Why the Caged Bird Sings*, *Gather Together in My Name* and *Heart of a Woman*, and of five collections of poetry.

LYNDA BARRY is a cartoonist and writer whose published works include *The Good Times Are Killing Me* (which was also adapted for the stage), *Down the Street*, *The Fun House*, *Big Ideas* and *Girls and Boys*. She has been a guest commentator on National Public Radio's *All Things Considered* and her illustrations frequently appear in national publications such as *Savy*, *Harpers* and *Esquire*.

ALISON BECHDEL grew up in rural Pennsylvania and attended Oberlin College, where she came out in 1979. She moved to New York City after graduating and it was there that the first "Dykes To Watch Out For" cartoon was published in the 1983 Lesbian Pride issue of *Womanews*. Three collections of her cartoons—*Dykes to Watch Out For*, *More Dykes to Watch Out For*, and *New, Improved! Dykes to Watch Out For*—as well as a yearly calendar have been published by Firebrand Books (141 The Commons, Ithaca, New York 14850).

MARY S. BELL, a Vassar College graduate now living in Honolulu, Hawaii, is both a painter and writer whose short stories and satirical pieces have been published in *The Key West Review* and *Exquisite Corpse*.

JENNIFER BERMAN'S cartoons have appeared in *In These Times*, *Vegetarian Times*, *Chicago Times* and *The Funny Times*. A catalog of T-shirts and postcards is available from Humerus Cartoons, Box 6614, Evanston, Illinois, 60204-6614.

JULIE BLACKWOMON lives in Philadelphia with two cats and her partner of six years, Brenda, who has promised to tell all to the *National Enquirer* unless her name is mentioned. Blackwomon has been published in *Lesbian Poetry*, *Lesbian Fiction*, *Painted Bride Quarterly* and *Home Girl's*. Thanks to Seal Press she will be featured this fall in *Voyages Out 2* and now has answers for strangers who ask with a touch of arrogance, "and what do you do?" Now at work on a novel, she has given up her hunt for disgruntled writers, willing to form a "I-hate-Joyce-Carol-Oates-and-other-prolific-writers," fan and envy club.

LISA BLAUSHILD's work has appeared in *Bomb* magazine, *Exquisite Corpse*, the *SoHo Arts Weekly*, and the anthology *Blatant Artifice*. Her play *Straight Talk* was performed at La Mama in New York.

ALICE BLOOM lives in Mt. Vernon, Maine, and teaches English at the University of Maine in Farmington. Her essays and reviews have appeared in *Yale Review*, *Hudson Review*, *Aegean Review*, *Harper's*, *Maine Progressive*, and others. She has recently completed a book-length collection of essays.

CLAIRE BRETECHER has published more than a dozen books in her native

France and in many other countries, including *Mothers, Frustration,* and *Still More Frustration.*

JENNIFER CAMPER lives in New York City and draws cartoons for *Outweek Magazine* and other publications brave enough to print her work. She vehemently denies those nasty rumors about her and the Rockettes on that sailboat last summer, and besides, she doesn't even own that many inner tubes.

MYRA CHANIN is
   (a) an ordinary person from Philadelphia
   (b) the most brilliant comic mind since Nostrodamus
   (c) both of these
   (d) neither of these

ROZ CHAST's cartoons frequently appear in *The New Yorker, Mother Jones* and *The Sciences.* Her books include *The Four Elements, Last Resorts, Unscientific Americans, Parallel Universes, Poems and Songs* and *Mondo Boxo.*

MAXINE CHERNOFF co-edits *New American Writing.* Her novel, *Plain Grief,* will be published by Simon & Schuster in 1991. *Bop,* her book of stories, received the LSU/Southern Review short fiction award for 1988. She is also the author of five books of poems, most recently *Leap Year Day: New and Selected Poems.*

Born in the joke butt state of New Jersey, CATHY CRIMMINS now lives in the hilarious city of Philadelphia, where she is a freelance writer. Her books include *The Official YAP Handbook, EntreChic,* and *The Secret World of Men.* She has written for *Redbook, Savvy, Working Woman, Success!, Philadelphia Magazine, Working Mother, The Village Voice,* and numerous newspapers and journals. Her first novel is due some time this century.

DEBRA HOFFMAN DECKER was born in Pennsylvania, but spent much of her adult life coast-hopping between California and the east. A teacher by profession, she decided while undergoing a mid-life crisis, that she really wanted to write. To this end she has studied playwriting at HB Studio in New York City, and more recently has pursued the poetry muse. Her haiku have been published in *Haiku Headlines* and *Brussles Sprout,* and several longer poems have appeared in *Up Against the Wall, Mother* ... Presently she is living in Bethlehem, Pennsylvania and commuting to New York regularly, where she is working on her MFA in Playwriting at Brooklyn College. Her goal: Broadway (or at least off-off Broadway).

DONNA DECLUE "I'm 43 years old and live on five acres in a rural area near Sarasota, Florida, with my husband Greg and our two sons, Nathan, 6, and Colin, 9 months. I grew up in Columbia, Missouri, and attended the University of Missouri, majoring in English, back when colleges were offering really good liberal arts educations. That's why I've been able to work as a secretary all my life. I've been writing for pleasure for about two years, and this is my first published work."

N. LEIGH DUNLAP is a two-time winner of the International Gay and Lesbian Press Association's "Outstanding Achievement" Award and the author of two book collections: *Morgan Calabresé: The Movie;* and *Run That Sucker at Six!!!.* The second book was a Lambda Literary Award nominee. Her weekly strip, *Morgan Calabresé,* is syndicated and appears regularly in ten papers around the U.S. She hopes to develop a "cartoonist-owned," professional syndicate for alternative and underground cartoonists, and urges all interested cartoonists to lend their energies to the effort. She resides in Northampton, Massachusetts, where, because cartooning is no way to make any kind of living, she and her lover are co-owners of a wholesale gourmet coffee roaster.

SHARONE EINHORN is a writer and cartoonist whose work appears regularly in *Avenue* and *Smart.*

NORA EPHRON is the author of *Heartburn, Crazy Salad* and *Wallflower at the Orgy.*

TAFFY FIELD graduated from the University of Pennsylvania in 1971, after receiving a fellowship to International College in Beruit, Lebanon. She has taught mathematics and creative writing to children. Currently, she teaches house-building at the Shelter Institute. Co-owner of the Center Street Grainery in Bath, Maine, Taffy lives by the banks of the Kennebec River. She has a son and a daughter. Her short story collection, *Short Skirts,* is available from The Dog Ear Press, 132 Water Street, Gardiner, ME 04345 for $9.95 + $1.50 postage.

POLLY FROST was born in 1952 in Pasadena, California, and grew up there and later in Santa Barbara. For a brief period she was a literature major before dropping out of UCSB. She began writing fiction at the age of thirty. She now lives with her husband in New York City and, in addition to humor, publishes journalism and is at work on a play.

ELLEN GRUBER GARVEY's recently completed collection of short stories is titled *Playing the Field at Camp Socialist Brooklyn and Other Stories.* Her work has appeared in feminist and literary magazines and collections, including two other Crossing Press anthologies.

KATE GAWF is currently residing in Italy where she is studying to start her own religion which she hopes will give her generous tax breaks. She retains an American P.O. box with a staff of tiny elves who answer mail and fill orders for postcards of her drawings. For mail order or other information write P.O. Box 5041, Portland, OR 97208.

VERONICA GENG is the author of *Partners* and *Love Trouble Is My Business.* She has been a writer and fiction editor at *The New Yorker* for ten years.

DIANE F. GERMAIN "I am a French-American Lesbian Feminist psychiatric social worker conducting a strength group for *Women Survivors of Incest and/or Childhood Molestation* which is over three and a half years old. I am one of the founding mothers of *Dykes on Hikes, The Lesbian Referral Service, Beautiful Lesbian*

Thespians, an early principal of *San Diego Lesbian Organization,* and a collective member of *Califia Community.* I create humor as a hedge against the misogyny of heterosexist phallocentric patriarchy and to tickle the Lesbians."

JEAN JEFFREY GIETZEN is a columnist for *Religion Teacher's Journal,* and has published in *McCall's Silver Edition, Reader's Digest, Catholic Digest,* and the *Milwaukee Journal & Sentinel.* "Have been writing since I was ten . . . received my first rejection from Metro Goldwyn Mayer in 1947. Kept on writing anyway. Have a small book of poetry out from Resource Publications *(A People Set Apart)* published in 1983. Teach creative writing at Concordia University in Mequon, WI. I'm married and have three grown children and will be a grandma soon. I smoke cigarettes, have a cocktail party every night before dinner and am still in love with my husband of 29 years."

NIKKI GIOVANNI, best-selling author of *Black Feeling, Black Talk, Black Talk/ Black Judgement, My House, The Women and the Men, Cotton Candy on a Rainey Day,* and *Those Who Ride the Night Winds,* lives in Cincinnati, Ohio. Among her many honors, she has been named Woman of the Year by *Ebony* magaizine.

MARY GRABAR gave birth to a son, Carson, but she did not take it like a man. "If Men Could Become Pregnant" originally appeared in *Southline,* a former Atlanta weekly newspaper. Mary Grabar's humor, feature articles and columns have appeared in *The Atlanta Journal-Constitution, Southline, The Progressive, Atlanta Business Chronicle, San Francisco Chronicle, The San Diego Union* and others. Her fiction has been published in *Catalyst.* She is currently working on a nonfiction book, which will be a feminist/historical analysis of motherhood. She is Yugoslavian by birth, but grew up in Rochester, New York. She has lived in Atlanta, Georgia since 1985.

EDITH GROSSMAN has only recently begun to publish her own poetry. A critic and translator of contemporary Latin American literature, her latest translations include Gabriel Garcia Márquez' *Love in the Time of Cholera* and *The General in His Labyrinth.* A resident of New York City, where Dr. Zizmor's ads fill the subway trains, she teaches at Dominican College.

MARY HAZZARD is the author of three novels and numerous plays. She has received an NEA fellowship in playwriting and spent 1988-89 as writer-in-residence at the College of William and Mary.

BOBBIE LOUISE HAWKINS is the author of *My Own Alphabet* (Coffee House Press), *One Small Saga* (Coffee House Press), *Back to Texas* (Bearhug), *Frenchy and Cuban Pete* (Tombouctou) and *Almost Everything* (Long River Books) among others. Winner of a NEA Fellowship, she currently teaches writing at Naropa Institute in Boulder.

JANET RUTH HELLER is an assistant professor of English at Nazareth College in Kalamazoo, Michigan. Her book, *Coleridge, Lamb, Hazlitt, and the Reader of Drama,* was recently published by the University of Missouri Press. Her poetry has appeared in *Anima, Cottonwood Review, Organic Gardening, Kentucky Poetry Review, Women: A Journal of Liberation, Lilith, Earth's Daughters, The Writer,* and *Modern Maturity.*

MARIAN HENLEY lives in Dallas, Texas, with an elderly black cat. Her weekly comic strip, "Maxine!," has appeared in the *San Francisco Chronicle,* the *Dallas Morning News, Whole Earth Catalog, Funny Times, Heavy Metal,* and various other books and publications in the U.S. and Sweden. In 1989, she was awarded a grant to produce two live-action videos based on the comic strip. Her graphic novel, *Maxine,* was published in 1987 by New American Library.

NICOLE HOLLANDER'S "Sylvia" strip is syndicated to 46 newspapers. Her work is collected in *Tales from the Planet Sylvia, The Whole Enchilada,* and others.

ALICE KAHN is the author of *Luncheon At the Cafe Ridiculous, My Life As a Gal* and *Multiple Sarcasm.* Born in the midwest, schooled in New York, and living in the West, she is a self proclaimed "broad with a broad perspective." She lives in Berkeley, California.

CHARLOTTE AVRUTIS KELLAR is a native New Yorker whose work has been published in the *New York Times* and the *Sunday Magazine* section of the *New York Daily News.*

MARY LAWTON is a California based cartoonist. Her works have appeared in a variety of publications including *The Realist,* and the *Utne Reader.* She is currently working on a children's book, *The Uncomfortable Bug in a Rug,* and editing a book of women's humorous "hair stories," which she will also illustrate. She makes her living in freelance animation and is secretly fascinated by the quirks and personal habits of others.

FRAN LEBOWITZ is the author of *Metropolitan Life* and *Social Studies.*

DIANE LEFER's short fiction has appeared in literary journals including *The Agni Review* and *Boulevard* and in national magazines ranging from *Black Belt* to *Vogue.* She has read from her work at venues such as the Library of Congress, the National Arts Club and a now-defunct cabaret club called *The Dive.*

RACHEL LODEN's poems have been published in *Poet & Critic, Beloit Poetry Journal* and *Southern Review,* among other magazines. She lives in Palo Alto, California.

MERRILL MARKOE is the editor of *Late Night With David Letterman: The Book.*

PATRICIA MARX "I've written three books—*How to Regain Your Virginity* (with Charlotte Stuart), *You Can Never Go Wrong By Lying,* and *Blockbuster* (with Douglas McGrath). I've also written a play—*Dominoes* (with Douglas McGrath). I've been a staff writer for Saturday Night Live and many other shows, including several Children's Television Workshop shows. My work's been in the *New York Times, The Atlantic* and *The New Yorker* (I write Talk of The Towns). I'm a contributing editor of *Spy*. I write mostly humor because I'm too shallow to write anything else. I teach humor writing at the New School. I'm writing a screenplay."

CANDYCE MEHERANI, a widely published humor writer, is working on a novel. (But who isn't?) She is the owner of Aloka Gallery, an art gallery specializing in visionary art from around the world. Basically, she is just trying to amuse herself until the mother ship arrives to take her back to Uranus.

MARY MOLYNEUX'S work has appeared in *Telephone, The Alternative Press,* and other literary magazines. *Lessons For a Fourth Grade Class,* a collection of her poems, is available from The Toothpaste Press. She was the singer in a band called *Tall Men Who Hop,* now (unfortunately) defunct.

ALEXANDRA MORGAN was born in Memphis, Tennessee and grew up in the orange groves of Covina, California. After studying at the Juilliard School of Acting, she completed her B.A. in Humanities at the University of Southern California. She was a founding member of Los Angeles' seminal experimental theatre group, "The Company Theatre," where she wrote, acted, and produced for four years. She has performed in over 50 plays in New York, San Francisco, and Los Angeles. Her fiction has appeared in *The Southern California Anthology.* She is currently finishing her master's degree in Professional Writing at U.S.C., completing a collection of short stories, and writing lyrics with Brian Wilson for his upcoming solo album. Her play, *Daughter DeLuxe,* recently won the Ninth Annual One-Act Play Festival at U.S.C.

ANDREA NATALIE'S panel, "Stonewall Riots," appears regularly in numerous lesbian/gay publications throughout the country. Her first book of cartoons, *Stonewall Riots,* is now available at bookstores. She also publishes "Lesbian Cartoonists' Network," a newsletter.

LESLÉA NEWMAN is the author of seven books, including *A Letter To Harvey Milk, Heather Has Two Mommies,* and *Secrets.* She was voted the class wit of her high school in 1973. Currently she lives in Western Massachusetts with the woman she loves and their two cats. Her newest book, *Gloria Goes to Gay Pride,* will be published by Alyson Publications in 1991.

SHARON NIEMCZYK "These pieces are part of a series in which I combined images from ads in old magazines with my own interpretive titles to reveal their sexist context or change their meanings entirely."

"Careful, honey, he's anti choice" was part of "The 1984 Show" at the Ronald Feldman Gallery in New York City (1983), and has been published in *Ms., Heresies,* and *The Village Voice.* My primary art form is now animation and I enjoy teaching many children throughout Oregon how to make their own animated films. Postcards of "Careful, honey" are available through FeMail Art Productions, P.O. Box 10706, Portland, OR 97210, and T-shirts/posters through Northern Sun Merchandising, 2916 E. Lake St., Minneapolis, MN 55406, (612) 729-2001.

ELLEN ORLEANS is a writer, graphic artist and lesbian organizer. Author of "Can't Keep A Straight Face," a monthly humor column in *Quest Magazine* (Denver), she also writers for *Booklook,* a children's publication. With one completed short story and two novels in the works, she divides her writing time between fiction, non-fiction and occasional letters to friends. Ellen lives in boulder with her partner Lori Fuller with whom she strives to lead an ecologically-correct, bio-degradable life.

PAMELA PAINTER's stories have appeared or are forthcoming in: *Atlantic, Boston Globe Magazine, Chicago Magazine, Confrontation, Epoch, Harper's, Kenyon Review, Mademoiselle, North American Review, Ploughshares, Redbook, Sewanee Review, Special Report, Threepenny Review, Transatlantic Review, Virginia Quarterly Review,* among others. Her short story collection, *Getting To Know the Weather,* published by University of Illinois Press in 1985, won the 1986 Great Lakes College Association (GLCA) Award for New Fiction.

HELEN PEPPE was born in Auburn, Maine, in 1967. On high school graduation, she moved to Portland where she attended and graduated *summa cum lauda* in English literature from the University of Southern Maine in May 1990. She won first place in a University short story contest in April 1990, and she has had poems and short stories published nationally in magazines and anthologies. She is currently a freelance writer and lives in South Portland, Maine, with her husband.

LAURIE PIKE, originally from Cincinnati, now lives in New York where she edits the annual *Gutter Poodles* fiction compilation. Her nonfiction articles have appeared in *Vanity Fair, The Face, Spin* and *Egg.*

EVELYN ROEHL is the author of *Whole Food Facts* (Healing Arts Press, Rochester, Vermont) and former managing editor of the *North Country Anvil* magazine. Her writings have also appeared in *Iowa Woman, Tidewater, What We Will, Zeitgeist, Faminews, The Scoop, The Winonan,* and *PCC Sound Consumer.* She founded and edited *YUM! Your Usable Magazine* for three years and is currently owner-operator of Flying Fingers Typing & Graphics in Seattle, Washington.

MIRIAM SAGAN has published poetry, fiction, and essays in over 150 magazines inthe U.S., England, Canada, and Japan. She holds a B.A. from Harvard University and an M.A. in creative writing from Boston University. Among her dozen published collections are the poetry book *Aagean Doorway* (Zepher, 1984), the tape cassette *Spilling Marmalade* (Pectin Audio, 1988), and the fiction chapbook, *Paths to the Nudist Beach* (Samisdat, 1989). She has been an artist is residence with the state of New Mexico and teaches ongoing classes in Santa Fe. The majority of her published work is lifted straight from her notebooks.

LORRAINE SCHEIN is a New York poet, science fiction writer and part-time anarchist whose work has appeared in *Heresies, Exquisite Corpse, and Semiotext(e)*

SF, among others. Her story "The Chaos Diaries" was included in *Memories and Visions* and her poetry in the anthology *If I had a Hammer: Women's Work in Poetry, Fiction and Photography*.

CINDY SCHUMOCK lives and works as a graphic production manager in Portland, Oregon. Co-founded in 1980 FeMail Art Productions, a feminist artists' group dedicated to furthering positive images of women through postcard publishing and distribution.

CAROL SIBLEY is a freelance writer who has written an amusing, poignant book about her ten years of experiences as a Girl Scout Leader.

NINA SILVER, ever since finding her clitoris, has been more relaxed. Her fiction, poetry, and essays on sexuality (what else?), feminism, the natural sciences, new wicca and spirituality have been published in numerous anthologies and magazines in the United States and abroad. She is currently working on a full-length book, *A Gateway Through the Channel*.

MARCIA STEIL is a commercial writer based in Chatsworth, California. She completed college after her two daughters were born, taught nursery school, junior high, and high school, drove up to 6 carpools at a time, became a technical editor, and, at 40, started her own writing business and published several articles for business magazines. This is her first published fiction. She is still married to her first husband, Bill, whom she met when he was her eighth grade paper boy in Ames, Iowa, and who didn't like her very much. He likes her better now.

NOREEN STEVENS is a comic artist living and working in Winnipeg, Manitoba, Canada. When not cartooning she is desperately trying to learn to juggle and do cool things with a yoyo. She cites the trauma of a suburban childhood as her source of strength and inspiration. She says "There are lots of cartoons about suburbia, and lots of cartoons about lesbians. What I want to look at are the untold thousands of lesbians with one foot in the Land of White Bread and the other in a pair of Birkenstocks."

FLEUR WINNECOUR TAMON of San Antonio, Texas, has been married 46 years to war hero Harvey Tamon, has 3 grown children and 1-1/3 grandchildren, and has had 25 fiction and nonfiction pieces published.

A.J. TOOS has published cartoons in *Cosmopolitan, Complete Woman* and a number of other magazines and newspapers. She lives in Washington, DC with three cats.

Conceptual humorist ARIEL TRAMWAY is currently seeking NEA funding for her multi-media presentation "Suck My Dick, Jessie Helms!"
SUSAN TROTT lives in Mill Valley, California. She is the author of seven novels, the latest of which is *The Exception*.

ROSALIND WARREN is a bankruptcy attorney, a feminist and a mother. Her short fiction has been published in numerous magazines from *Seventeen* to *Beatniks in Space*, and in many anthologies. She received a 1990 Commonwealth of Pennsylvania Council on the Arts fellowship in literature.

IRENE WARSAW of Bay City, Michigan, has two books of humorous poetry in print: *A Word In Edgewise* and *Warily We Roll Along*. Hundreds of her poems have been published in hundreds of magazines like *Saturday Evening Post, Wall Street Journal, The Atlantic* and *Good Housekeeping*.

CHOCOLATE WATERS has written and published three books of poems, short stories and cartoons, and her work has appeared in hundreds of literary magazines and newspapers. She was recently awarded a grant from the Money for Women/Barbara Deming Memorial Fund, Inc. to complete her latest book, *Chocolate Waters in Trilogy: I Was A Closet Woman, Chocolate and the World, Chocolate Comes of Age*. On being asked how she got her name, she says, "I was born Miss Waters, but I decided to like chocolate." Chocolate Waters lives and writes in Manhattan.

DEBRA RIGGIN WAUGH lives with her dog and two cats in Tacoma Park, Maryland, and is often free for lunch. While (semi-) patiently waiting for Ed McMahon to deliver that multi-million dollar check, Debra spends her spare time working full-time as a writer/editor on AIDS education and looking for a nearby place to swim naked. Her work has also appeared in *Word of Mouth: Short-Short Writings by Women* and *I Had A Hammer: Women's Work in Poetry and Fiction*.

JULIA WILLIS is a transplanted Southerner living in Boston. Having made the transition from video artist and stand-up performer to sit-down writer, she is the recipient of a 1988-89 fiction fellowship from the Massachusetts Artists Foundation; her short stories have appeared in national publications that include *Bostonia, Triquarterly,* and *The Roberts Writing Awards Annual*. Her humor book, *Who Wears the Tux?*, was published by Banned Books in 1990. A one-act play, "Going Up," is anthologized in *Places, Please!* (Spinsters/Aunt Lute Books, 2nd edition, 1988), and she writes comedy material for Joan Rivers. Julia says, "I suppose you could say my past is checkered. It's certainly been fun."

IRENE ZAHAVA owns Smedley's Bookshop in Ithaca, New York. She has edited fifteen anthologies of stories by women, published by The Crossing Press, including *Word of Mouth* (short-short stories), *My Father's Daughter, My Mother's Daughter* and *Through Other Eyes: Animal Stories by Women*.

ZANA "I'm 44, disabled, Jewish, and have lived on lesbian land for the past 11 years. As far as I'm concerned, lesbian culture is the most exciting thing happening in the universe—but we're not perfect and being able to laugh at our foibles helps me deal with the hard parts."

The Crossing Press
publishes a full selection of
feminist titles.
To receive our current catalog,
please call — Toll Free — 800/777-1048.